FOREWORD

I was 14-years-old the first time I heard KJ-52. It was 2002, and my parents had owned a Christian book store at the time. I distinctly remember receiving a "not for resale" copy of Collaborations. On the front cover, I saw an earring clad white guy with frosted tips. On the back cover, I saw features from Thousand Foot Krutch and Pillar, two rap/rock bands I loved at the time. I even saw the names John Reuben and Ill Harmonics there. Needless to say, I knew this would be something I liked. I popped the CD into my stereo, jumped in the shower, and I was hooked.

Over the next few years, KJ-52 would be the soundtrack to my youth group days. "Dear Slim 1 & 2," "KJ Five Two," all of Peace of Mind and Behind the Musik, would be in constant rotation wherever I went. KJ had, and still has, this uncanny ability to hit you with something incredibly detailed and powerful. He can paint the picture of a story in a digestible way without concerning himself with "lyrical- miracles" or without watering down the message. He can also make you laugh hysterically with out of left field songs and isn't afraid to bring humor to his music. This is something I always appreciated and hoped to emulate when I began creating my own music. As a teenager, it's always hard to be yourself and fit in. That's why KJ has been so instrumental to generations of young people - he's never been afraid to be authentically him.

Flash forward many years and now I'm a journalist. I get to interview artists for a living. Naturally, I knew I had to get KJ-52, and in 2014 I got to speak to him for the first time. Move a couple of years later and I'm now working for Rapzilla. I interviewed him again, and this time it was different. There was a lot of good chemistry on the call, and I could now relate to KJ as an adult rather than me looking up to him as a kid. It was a cool experience. Your favorite artists are just like you. We linked up again for a few more interviews, story ideas, and podcasts over the next few years. We even got to kick it in Newark, NJ for a few hours. KJ shared countless stories from a nearly 25-year career. He imparted wisdom with everything from tricks of the trade, how to win a crowd, best and worst shows, failures and success, and on and on.

Then, at some point last year, he approached me with the idea of writing a book. I thought it was a brilliant idea. He wanted me to help him write it. I didn't even hesitate for a second. There were a number of false starts, stop and goes, and rethinking, but now here we are. Ultimately, I didn't "write the book" per se, but I did what I do best with KJ - talk. We kicked around story ideas and I provided the listening ear and conversational tone that KJ was trying to convey in the book. Some of these stories I had heard before, some of these stories shocked me, and some of the stories were just for me. Overall, it was an amazing experience.

So to those reading this book, know that every story you read in this book is from a genuine guy who loves the Lord, his family, and serving people. Through all the trials of life, music, and oddly enough, people shooting at him, KJ-52 has had a longer career than at least 95% of his peers. He's faced the highs and lows of Christian music fame, the vigors of life, and he's still standing.

And to Jonah "KJ-52" Sorrentino, my early music hero, favorite story collaborator, and my friend; thank you for letting me be part of your journey. I'm forever grateful and honored to have helped with this, and am inspired by your passion.

"One love, One God, One Way."

Justin Sarachik
Editor-in-Chief of Rapzilla.com

I love to hear a good story. One of my favorite story tellers is KJ-52. I've known this guy for over twenty years and he's had me laughing ever since I met him. He has traveled extensively and found himself in lots of interesting situations with lots of interesting characters. His sense of humor, combined with his insight and experience always have me excited to hear about his latest adventure.

He has this gift to remember random things that are hilarious. I've heard some of the stories from his new book and I can tell you that you won't be disappointed.

Tommy "Urban D."Kyllonen
Pastor, Hip-Hop Artist, Author

Copyright © 2019 Jonah Sorrentino
52 Publishing
P.O. Box 150415
Cape Coral, FL 33915-0415

All Rights Reserved.

No part of this book may be reproduced in any form without written permission from 52 Publishing.

Written by: Jonah Sorrentino (kj-52)
Edited by: Andrew Schwab
Interviewed by: Justin Sarachik
Additional Proofing by: Stephen Bontz
Book Design by: Edward 'spe©' Bayonet | @iambayonet

"What Happened Was" is available in Print, Digital and Audio formats.

ISBN: 9781096673187 (print)

Printed in the United States of America

www.kj52.com • kj52@kj52.com

 @kj52instagram

 @kj52

 @kj52

This book is dedicated to
Christa, Jacob, Isaiah and James.
I love you with all of my heart!
- Love Jonah/Dad

This intro and conclusion are going to be the only things I'm actually going to write in this book. You may be saying "hold up.. how is he saying this is the only thing he's going to write? Aren't I about to read a book written by Kj?" The truth is writing is super hard for me, my brain moves at a pace that typing can't catch up to.

Blame it on a short attention span or a fast moving brain I don't know, but I am a chronic over thinker/over analyzer. My brain + communication process is wired toward a live crowd. I need to see faces, I need to see whether or not the whole thing is connecting, I need to know if its working (there's probably some deep seated need for attention in there some therapy session would reveal). Writing doesn't come easy for me because there is no immediate feedback, I have no idea how or if the content is working. You may say "How is that possible when he's written songs for 25 plus years?" Great question..

Song writing is a whole other skill set, but it's also a skill set where I can have bad grammar, run on sentences, typo's, slurred words and much more in my lyrics and nobody bats an eye (especially in hip hop).

This is why it's taken me this long to do a book… this had been on the docket for a long time.

I can talk all day (talking has never been a problem) but you drop me in front of a laptop and say "TYPE!" and I'm in struggleville. Years of frustration and starting and stopping helped me to finally figure out how to crack the code! Want to know how I did it?

It started with a conversation with a long time friend, I told them "tell me some stuff you remember from way back when… what stories ring true in your mind?" One conversation turned into another and they all seemed to start with the phrase what happened was...

I started compiling all of those stories into a journal, every time I'd come up with one I'd jot it down until I had pages and pages of "what happened was…" type stories. I then sent them off to the homie Justin Sarachik and just sent him a list of the story titles. I said "based on what you see.. tell me which one of these titles makes you intrigued?"

He'd pick the stories, we'd hop on the phone and then I'd tell him the story while I was standing in front of the microphone recording the audio (told you I need an audience). Suddenly the whole thing became the easiest creative endeavor I'd ever done.

I would then take the audio, transcribe it to text and then send it off to another homie Andrew Schwab who would re-edit that into a readable format. He'd then send it back and I'd do a final edit (after running the story by anyone that might be in the story and getting Stephen the intern to do a final typo proof) and that's what you're about to read.

This book should feel like a conversation between me and you because that's literally what it is. It's not a tell all/gossip book, my only two requirements of any story that I included was: is it positive and does it have a resolution? This book is a testament to what God can do with a misfit. I hope you have as much enjoyment reading it as I did "writing" it.

love you guys,

Jonah.

TABLE of CONTENTS

pg.04	Foreword
pg.06	Copyright
pg.07	Dedication
pg.08	Introduction
pg.10	Chapter 1 How I Got My Name
pg.14	Chapter 2 Insecure
pg.18	Chapter 3 Tron the Racist Dog
pg.22	Chapter 4 I Almost Burned The Island Down
pg.28	Chapter 5 The G-Force Posse
pg.34	Chapter 6 I Almost Became a Mormon
pg.38	Chapter 7 How I Wrote My First Rap
pg.42	Chapter 8 Prophecy Fulfilled
pg.46	Chapter 9 Gun Shots on MLK
pg.50	Chapter 10 Booed Off the Stage at Tribe Called Quest
pg.54	Chapter 11 They Put Me On the Gang File
pg.58	Chapter 12 Wedding Day Disaster
pg.62	Chapter 13 How I Was Discovered
pg.66	Chapter 14 Spells, Warlocks and Skate Kids
pg.70	Chapter 15 Dear Slim
pg.76	Chapter 16 Scribble Jam
pg.80	Chapter 17 Dove Awards
pg.84	Chapter 18 Christian Rap Beef
pg.88	Chapter 19 Jesus Freak
pg.92	Chapter 20 Bill Cosby's Bathroom
pg.98	Chapter 21 Agree to Disagree
pg.104	Chapter 22 Guinness World Record Holder
pg.108	Chapter 23 Mary vs Martha
pg.112	Chapter 24 Q & A + Quotes
pg.118	Conclusion
pg.120	Gallery
pg.126	Thank You's

CHAPTER 1
HOW I GOT MY NAME.

I'M STILL VERY PASSIONATE ABOUT CAKE TO THIS DAY...

"I wanted to name you Sky..."
~ Lana (KJ's mom)

Soundtrack to this story: Kjfivetwo (Pronounced Five Two LP)

My name has been a point of contention for me for most of my life. By the time I reached junior high, my insecurity about it reached an apex, mainly because people couldn't pronounce it correctly. People called me Joanna...Joshua...Johann. When I became a Christian, kids would tease me and call me Jehovah. When you are a teenager, you just want to fit in. And if you have an odd first name, most kids have the option to fall back on your middle name. In my case, I didn't have this option because my middle name is Kirsten, which...uh...is a girl's name.

My full name is Jonah Kirsten Carlin Sorrentino. So, I really had zero options. I had a Hebrew name, a Scottish name, a Sicilian name, or a girl's name to pick from. It was just the worst possible scenario you can imagine when you hit a time where you just don't want to stand out. My whole entire life, I had never met another person named Jonah. People would make references to the story in the Old Testament, and to be honest, that was the only Bible story I knew because I didn't grow up in a church-based home.

To give you some further context for this story, I should mention that my home wasn't very conventional. I called my parents by their first name probably up until about ten years ago. I was raised to call them by their first names because my parents wanted for us to be on equal footing. I didn't know any different. I grew up thinking everyone did that. I found out years later my mom almost named me Sky. Her side of the family was very much into boating, sailing and the like. My dad's side of the family is from Jersey. Both of my parents were artistic people. They could not agree on a name for me, and up to the moment I was born, they had not landed on a name and their idea was..." well, we'll just name him later after we bring him home."

"I still put my hand on my hip and look this awkward"

So I was born, and the doctor insisted that they had to name me. So apparently, they asked the doctor, for a name he hadn't heard in a long time. I find it interesting that they wanted to go with a name that was uncommon. To me, it seemed like from the moment I was brought into the world, the whole purpose was that I would not be like everybody else. When you just wanted to blend in (ie. when you're twelve) that's when it became a real noticeable problem for me.

In hindsight, my name has defined everything about who I am. There has never been anything typical about who I am, I wear that like a badge of honor these days. I'm proud of the uniqueness of how I was raised. I'm proud of all the perspectives I've seen. But you can only appreciate these things in hindsight. You never have that kind of perspective when you're trying to walk it out in the moment.

So, the doctor said Jonah was a name he hadn't heard in a long time. And for some reason, it clicked for my parents. Again, there wasn't any religious reference in their minds. And as my dad explains it, a year later they were driving through Amish country. They stopped somewhere, and I was in the backseat crying because I didn't like to be staying still (big surprise right?). Then, an Amish couple actually stopped them and said, "Hey, what's the baby's name?"

They said, "Jonah."

And the Amish couple said, "That boy will be a preacher someday...listen to those lungs!"

That story kind of blows my mind.

Another cool fact: my dad actually told me that they recorded my first sound. Meaning when I was born, he was there with a tape recorder to capture the first things that came out of my mouth. So, I look back on these things and have to conclude I was meant to be unique, and I was meant to be on the microphone.

One more interesting element to my story is the fact that, in a lot of ways, I ran from God. I ran from him for most of my adolescence. I ran from my calling, so to speak, just like the biblical Jonah, who also did something incredibly unique. Most prophets spoke to the Jews, and yet Jonah's calling was to go to the Gentile enemies and call for them to change. But he ran from his unique calling. And even the way God got his attention inside of his running was very unique. I can't help but draw some really interesting parallels and feel a kinship to them.

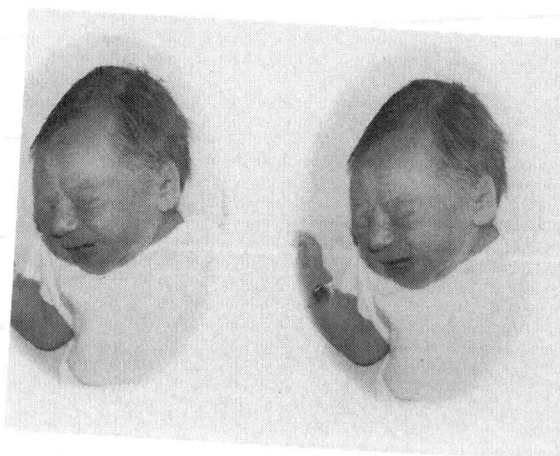

NO I'M NOT A TWIN...

But again, I was very embarrassed by my name. In Junior High, one of my good friends started calling me "Bones" because Jonah rhymed with Bonah, and Bonah became Bones. For most of my adolescence this name stuck with me. So, when I became a "DJ" (That's in quote because I never was an actual DJ, I just pretended like I could scratch on a single turntable in the living room), naturally, my name became DJ Bones. To this day, you know that friend of mine still calls me bones.

When I started rapping, for the life of me I could not come up with a good name, because there was nothing cool about Jonah. I didn't want to go with my name, and it was a rite of passage to have a rap name back then. I remember messing around on my folder one time in school, just sketching bubble letters, and I wrote "King J." That name sounded large to me back then, for some reason. Then, I added the "Mack." So, "King J Mack" was my initial moniker. At the time, the "Mack" part was a real easy way to have a rap name. For example, if your name was John, "J Mack" could have been your rap name.

NOTHING LIKE ROCKING A SUNDAY SCHOOL TO PUT THINGS IN PERSPECTIVE...

So, I liked "King J Mack," but I soon realized it was way too long. And it didn't write very well from a spelling standpoint. And, the worst part about it, was if I ever found myself in a battle, Mack rhymed with wack. Right off the bat I was in trouble, so my initial rap name only really lasted for about a year or so. When I hooked up with Goldin Child, I remember talking to Dax from Tunnel Rats who out of the blue said "I'm not going to call you King J Mack. I'm going to call you KJ."

That stuck with me. It was obvious to me that KJ was a shorter, easier name to say. Then, for no particular reason, the number five-two popped in my head. There was literally nothing particular about it, no reason that number stuck out to me. Then, I remember going to Goldin Child's house as we were formulating our first group and I said, "Hey, from now on, I'm going to go by KJ52."

He asked, "What does that mean?"

I said, "I have no idea, but I'm going to go with it."

EVERYONE THOUGHT I WAS A CHAD BASED ON THIS PIC.

It wasn't until years later, when I got a record deal, that I attempted to attach meaning to it. So I looked up the numbers five and two, and that led me to the story of when Jesus took the five loaves and two fish then he multiplied it. The story really resonated with me because I don't have a lot to offer, but I try to give Christ everything I have. Even if I just feel like even if what I have is just a little, I know he will multiply it. I use that as a way to keep myself focused, keep myself humble, and keep myself in the right state of mind.

If you flash forward years later, while I was working on the documentary movie about my life, I found a drawing I did when I was very young. I had drawn a sailboat and for no particular reason, I wrote the number five-two on the sailboat. I must have done this when I was about four or five. So out of all the numbers, why would I pick those two numbers? Right? I suddenly realized why, in that moment of looking at the picture, I realized why I put five two on there - it's because five and two is a balanced number. Meaning, the way I drew it, I made the five as an inverse of the two. They mirrored one another, in other words.

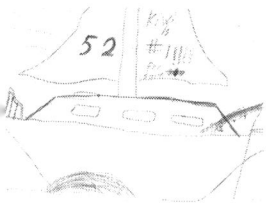

When I used to draw, everything had to be balanced and symmetrical. If I did something on one side, I had to balance it with the other side. And I realized one of the reasons why I picked KJ52 was because deep in my subconscious mind, that number was a balanced number. And I didn't even realize it until about two years ago. Nothing about my life has ever been typical, normal or easy and I have to say I'm glad God orchestrated it that way.

How I Got My Name | 13

CHAPTER 2
INSECURE

PARTING MY HAIR DID NOTHING TO FIX MY FRO!..

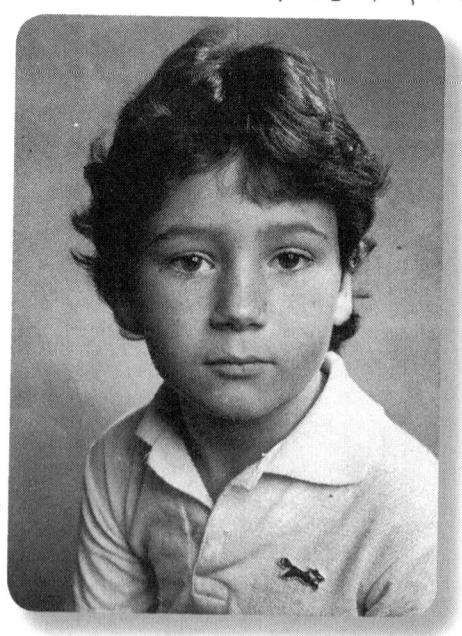

"Can I be honest, can I be real?"
~ kj52

Soundtrack to this chapter: "Napoleon Dynamite" kj52
(from the Behind the musik deluxe LP)

A s I was getting ready to work on this book, I was actually in the bathroom coloring the grey out of my hair. I sat there for a minute, and I looked up at myself and I realized my hair has always been a weird metaphor for all the things that I've been insecure about. I say that because I've never actually been able to do anything significant with my hair. I have this sort of bizarre, wavy, curly, bushy won't lay down, won't stand up in certain places, head of hair. I didn't think too much about it as a kid, but my parents really never cut my hair. In all of my school pictures, my hair is just some massive out of control thing on my head.

It wasn't until my junior high years that it became an issue, when everybody was doing the eighties perm or the spiky mullet rat tail cut I was stuck with this hair God gave me. I just wanted to be the kid that could fit in, but my hair literally wouldn't do any of it. I couldn't spike it up because it was too curly and wavy. I couldn't lay it down, because it was too unruly. I couldn't even do the 80's mullet or rat tail because it curled up all the way in the back. I tried everything. I tried Gel, I tried laying it down, and I tried putting it in a hat. My hair just said no.

In some ways my hair was really linked to the issue of me finally becoming secure in who I was and the way that God had made me.

Now, I was not a Christian at the time (junior high), so there really wasn't anything to build security in my life. Many things in my life were very much in flux, and very much in turmoil. But, as I embraced who Christ was at fifteen, I began to pour over scripture and begin to read God's truth over and over. The verse that began to stick out to me is the one that references the idea that there's a friend who sticks closer than a brother. However as my hair pertains to hip-hop culture, this became a problem because in a lot of ways I had to disguise my whiteness. In fact, coming up doing shows in south Florida, the highest compliment I could ever have gotten was for someone to say, Hey, are you Cuban or Puerto Rican?

As a rapper you really weren't allowed to rock a white boy haircut in the 90's, so the cut that I had to get by de-facto to blend in was the fade. Thank God, Goldin Child was learning how to cut hair back then. So he always gave me a really nice fade. If I had a tan, a fade, and a goatee, I could easily pass for Hispanic. I didn't really ever try to pass myself off as that, but if I could just make people do a double take, it was enough to essentially give me just one more opportunity to be accepted.

I had no other option than to get my hair cut every three-four weeks to keep that hairstyle looking right. But, for the first time in my life, I didn't have to do anything else besides that. My hair did exactly what I wanted it to do. It just sat there. If you see most pictures of me, for most of my life and most of my career, it's always been that short-cropped cut. Because of that, it requires that I don't have to do anything. So, I've had that haircut for a very long time.

THIS WAS AT CHRISTMAS, THE SHADOW MAKES IT LOOK LIKE I HAD A GUMBY CUT.--

I remember at one time, right before my collaborations album photo shoot, for no particular reason, I decided to get some highlights. In hindsight, it made no sense. And, of course, Goldin Child, my barber for life, handled it for me. I came out looking like a speckled hen. Todd Collins, my producer at the time, told me that if I wanted to be accepted by the Christian music industry I would have to grow my hair out. He said I couldn't look like a legitimate backpack rapper, that I had to look like a really acceptable white guy for middle America. So, it came back to my hair again, and I fought against that idea at first. But eventually I grew it out anyway, and I did the silly compromises just to be accepted.

In many ways, most of what I've done for most of my life has been based on fear and insecurity. I have made many of my decisions out of fear of failure, or the fear of being poor, or the fear that everyone who doubted me would be proven right. I have even made decisions because I was afraid all my insecurities about my own appearance would be proven right. Many of those decisions sadly made me forget what God has for me or what he has told me about who I really am. It has taken me years to finally be comfortable in my own skin, to be completely honest.

And I was thinking about all of this in light of the fact that I finally have really embraced who I am. I am a little goofy. I'm a little serious. I'm very hip hop, but I'm also very pop, and it took me most of my adulthood to finally get to this point. I say all this with the idea in mind that ten minutes ago I was staring into a mirror and putting Just For Men into my hair.

So, no one knows that I have grey hairs because now I'm on the other side of the "procedure."

I'm a guy pushing my mid-forties still doing a genre that is primarily for the youth. And, I am still taking steps to throw you off the scent again, whether that's dying the grey out of my hair, or keeping it cut short. In order to look younger, I also keep my facial hair cut short.

And I'll be honest, some of this is just really about being able to play the proper role. I understand, just like anyone else, I have to "put the suit on" before I do my job. Of course, there's still a part of me that struggles with all the same insecurities. Those insecurities on one hand, make me great, and on the other hand continue to dog me and try to keep me from seeing who Christ really should be in my life. Does that mean I am going to let the grey come back in my hair anytime soon? Absolutely not. What it does mean is that these things serve to remind me to dive deep into God's word to understand who I am. I am fearfully and wonderfully made. And the uniqueness of who I am is a beautiful thing to be celebrated, to never be downplayed, and to be completely embraced.

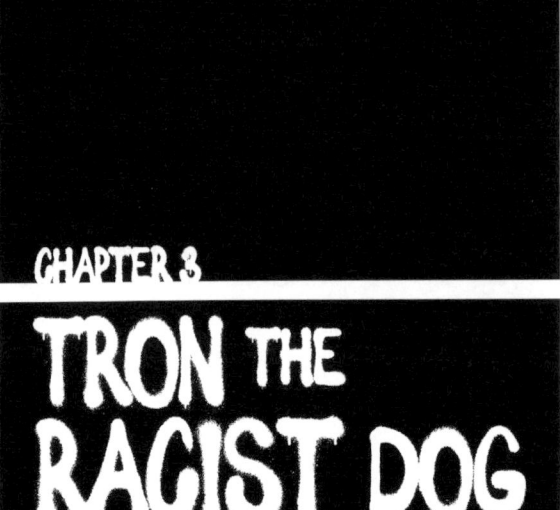

CHAPTER 3
TRON THE RACIST DOG

THIS IS WHERE WE LIVED, ITS AN OFFICE COMPLEX NOW -- GO FIGURE

"I'm the dog fairy and I'm hear to grant you three wishes.." The Dog Fairy 1982

Soundtrack to this chapter: "Once in a Lifetime" by Talking Heads
(only cause my dad used to play it all the time)

When I was seven years old, I lived in Ybor City with my dad, which at the time was a very financially depressed part of Tampa, Florida. As far as I remember, I was the only white kid in my entire neighborhood. It's not that there weren't other white folks-there were a few-but they were all adults in their thirties or forties, and these are the artistic types who stood out like sore thumbs. So, to say I was a minority in my own community would be an understatement; I was the only kid who was not Cuban or African American. My best friend (who was Cuban) wasn't even from my neighborhood and was never even allowed to spend the night at my house because his parents were worried about the safety of my hood.

And I do mean "hood."

We lived in an apartment behind my dad's storefront, in the same space. And around this time, break-ins became a regular part of life for us. Usually, this would consist of my dad and I leaving for the afternoon, only to return to have the back door to the store kicked in and the place looted. To attempt to rectify this, my dad would hire various people from the community to sweep up and do odd jobs. The thinking was that if people from the neighborhood were employed there, by association everyone else would stop targeting us. I remember one guy he hired was named "Killer." The name alone should have been a fair warning to us, but my dad was so desperate to stop the rampant ransacking that he was willing to give almost anyone a shot. Well, Killer ended up casing the place, and though we could never prove it, we think he was one of the many people who ended up robbing us.

AN ARTICLE THEY PUBLISHED ON MY DAD & HIS STUDIO...

A particular memory sticks out in mind which represents this chapter in our lives. One night, my dad woke up and caught someone coming through the window of the shop. He screamed at the guy, and the would-be robber was so scared he screamed back, then fell backwards out of the window. Luckily, I was a heavy sleeper and didn't witness any of this first hand.

I only mention all of this to paint the picture that there were a lot of things working against us in the neighborhood. My dad's plan to hire neighborhood folks to befriend them failed to deter robberies. So, he had to go another route. He wasn't the type to own a gun, even though he would have been completely justified in doing so. He just wasn't into firearms, and in fact, I had never even shot a gun my entire life up until just a couple of years ago.

Tron the Racist Dog | 19

So because guns were off the table, he decided to get a dog instead. Only, he didn't just buy a Labrador or a Collie. He wanted a menacing animal who would sit in the doorway of the shop and really deter people who might have been thinking of ripping us off.

I'll never forget the day the dog fairy showed up at our studio. And I mean this literally-one of my dad's friends dressed up like an actual fairy to deliver our new pooch/monster. Can you imagine? Our neighborhood was composed of some characters, to say the least. This lady was committed to the costume and the character. When she came in she said, I'm the dog fairy and I'm here to grant you your wishes. She produced this crossbred German Shepherd-esque pup. He was basically a mutt with several different breeds running through him, but I guess he resembled a Shepherd the most. I remember he was tall. He grew up to be a very, big dog, and he had gigantic ears.

I need to remind you this was the eighties. And I was a kid who was obsessed with sci-fi. So, when my dad gave me permission to name the dog, naturally only one name came to mind:

Tron.

I loved (and still love) that movie. Don't get me wrong, he ended up becoming a great dog, all things considered. Really, my only memory of him acting out was when, every once in a while, he escaped off his leash and ran to the fish market next door. He would sneak in the back and roll around in the fish guts, then return to us reeking, drenched in chum.

Tron did have one distinctive, "unique" personality trait, however. We were in a high foot-traffic area, next to a parking lot and on the main drag next to all the shops and businesses. My dad would chain him up inside the store so his leash would only reach to the doorway and no further. Again, people of various ethnicities and backgrounds walked by the front of the shop all day, day in and day out. Most of the day, Tron just hung out inside of the store. But, you have to picture this: A white dude would walk by, and the dog would just sit there in the store. A Cuban guy would walk by, and the dog would just sit there. Puerto Rican guy would walk by, and the dog wouldn't pay him any mind...

THIS IS THE DOOR HE USED TO COME CHARGING OUT OF..

1710

But when a black guy would walk by, the dog would lose it's mind…roaring and snarling and galloping toward the door at top speed until the chain would yank him back, with fantastic, cartoonish violence, just as he hit the door way. And every time he did this, the guy he was going after would jump back absolutely terrified. Each and every "victim" would jump ten paces into the middle of the street, while Tron would just bark bloody murder for about a minute. Then, the dog would chill out and calmly strut back to the middle of the store to lay down again.

This would happen over and over again. So after a certain point, we had to ask ourselves…

Was Tron a racist dog?

It was kind of hard to ignore the facts: brown, brown, brown, white… nothing.

Then, every single time a black man strolled by…

BWAAAARRRAAAORRRAAARRGGGH!!!

It certainly wasn't like we were sicking him on anyone ever, especially not a specific race. Do you understand? We never did one single thing to instill this in him. And it was only African Americans he went after.

I guess that was the first time in my life that I became aware of racism as an actual thing in the world, strangely enough. I realized that people formulate opinions based on nothing more than the appearance of skin. And indirectly, because of that dog, my dad really did use the situation as an opportunity to teach me that all people have value. I learned you can't formulate a response about people based on the way they appear; each person is a unique individual with a colorless soul, so to speak. This was years before I became a Christian. I knew racism was wrong, I knew that my dog was wrong.

Ironically, right around the same time, I was attending a private, Catholic school and, I'll never forget it, to this day-they actually played a song that was titled "What Color is God's Skin?" I remember all of this very clearly; we sat down in the class and the teacher would play the song…What color is God's skin? Is it black, Brown, or yellow? Is it red? Is it white? Everyone's the same in the good Lord's sight.

Diversity… uniqueness… race. At age seven, I understood everyone is the same… and this was and is a beautiful thing.

In no small part due to Tron, the racist dog.

CHAPTER 4
I ALMOST BURNED THE ISLAND DOWN

NOT GONNA LIE THIS WAS A SWEET BODY GLOVE T-SHIRT I HAD ON..

"It has hurt my heart to know that such a dear friend experienced such intense hurt during what we all know are notoriously difficult developmental years. I had very little idea what social mayhem was going on behind the scenes, nor did I realize the internal struggle. In the simplest, most pure form, I just knew that I cared so much. I could only hope that by unlocking the natural gifts and talents he has always possessed, that someday things would turn around for Jonah. The island in so many ways represents generations of life experience and family. It is and always will be a precious adventure that embraces and binds those who adventure with her." ~ Amy (the girl in the story)

Soundtrack to this chapter: "Never Tear Us Apart" by INXS

My grandfather was a Scottish immigrant. His story is similar to Horatio Alger. I didn't know him (because he passed away when I was two), but all these years later I am still finding out things about his legacy. He came over at a very young age, ended up making all these crazy patents, and made a ton of money in the automotive industry. Somehow he was even involved with the first lunar landing.

MY GRANPA + GRANDMA LOOKED LIKE MOVIE STARS.

He semi-retired by age thirty-five, and bought an entire island up in northern Michigan. It was on Higgins Lake. He purchased it to be a summer getaway for his family, but also because he had a very entrepreneurial spirit. So, he bought it to develop, and then sell off the plots of land. And that is exactly what he did.

But my mom's side of the family held onto a small part of it, and they had a cabin on the corner of the island. Every summer we drove twenty-four hours, with my grandma and cousin, all the way up to northern, rural Michigan to live on this island. I know this sounds like something out of a book or a movie, but that is exactly what I did.

We started going up there when I was five. There wasn't really a lot of kids on the island, but there were these two sisters that I met, and I still stay in touch with to this day. Outside of my family, I have known them longer than anyone in my entire life.

I stopped visiting the island for many years after my parents split. I didn't make it back up there until sixth grade. My cousin (who, in a lot of ways, was like my brother growing up) and I would visit the island together back then. And like all kids that age, we started to get bored even with having an island all to ourselves. So, we started getting into all kinds of mischief. One year, we decided it would be the "summer of the dares." So, we basically dared each other to do things, and each dare would get bigger. We ate live fish, we jumped off the back of our boat, we attempted to waterski on anything we could find (chairs, rafts and I think we even pulled

NOT SURE IF I WAS MORE ENAMORED BY THE DOG OR BY THE GIRL, PROBABLY BOTH..

a table once). We did anything that normal, mischievous, middle school kids would do. I was really struggling with my identity at that time. I was unusually short because I hadn't hit my growth spurt yet. I was a late bloomer. I also had a major crush on the older sister from the island, but I was unable to get past my awkward shyness and resorted to over compensating with annoying goofiness. I was in a tailspin, and this was way before I came to Christ.

I Almost Burned The Island Down | 23

THIS IS THE VISUAL REPRESENTATION OF ME TRYING TO HARD.-

ME, MY COUSIN & MY YOUNGER COUSIN, DANG I HAD SOME LONG SPIDER LEGS!

    Seventh grade rolled around, and I actually started to come into my own. From growing up on the island, we were also growing up with kids all around the island on the mainland. And in a really bizarre way, we had a lifestyle that was very much like the book Lord of the Flies. We were just kids being kids by ourselves. You would have your own boat at thirteen, and you could literally go anywhere. And with little to no supervision, we just basically began to get into trouble. But, it was the kind of trouble where it was impossible to catch us in the act, as you may guess that can lead to a lot of attempts at mayhem.

    At that time, hip-hop became my everything. It became my identity. It was the same with my friends. Most of those kids had a lot of money, and we were just following what we saw the adults doing. This consisted of drinking as much as we could, partying as much as we could, and getting as many girls phone numbers as we could. We were kids gone wild.

    I had struggled with my identity so much that when I went back to the island that summer, I decided I was going to become a brand new person. So, the first group of kids I met, I told them my name was Chris, instead of Jonah. One of those two sisters who had known me very well wondered: your name's not Chris, what are you doing? Who is this person you're attempting to be, I don't know you. In a lot of ways she was the voice of reason that I wasn't trying to hear, she came from a traditional family structure with good parental supervision and had been given lots of talks about "what was right and what was wrong". They weren't participating in that island/party/boating lifestyle and so I had to make a choice of which group I was going to hang with. I was a lost soul, and in a lot of ways I was looking to find my own identity. I had a completely fake identity, and I began to go along with whatever the other kids were doing.

All of this brings me to the point of one really crucial night in my life, one that really could have gone the wrong way. A couple of houses down there was a boat club, and we had found a bunch of beer that some of the adults had just left sitting out. Remember, we were 120-pound jr. high kids. So, the alcohol hit our system quickly and we were drunk immediately. We were sloppy. And somehow in our drunken stupor we had started talking to some girls right in front of their boyfriends. Well, after we left they weren't very happy about it, and they came and found us on the other part of the island. All my friends and I were going to be staying the night. We were going to sleep out on the point. At any rate, these boyfriends threatened to come down from the boat club and beat us up.

I'll never forget this because half of our crew couldn't even stand up. The other half was ready to go out, rumble-style. At that moment, my cousin ran to the front of the house, flipped on the lights, and started yelling in the loudest voice he could. He told the boyfriends to get out of there, pretending to be an adult. It worked, and those guys ran off. And it was a weird moment from an eighties movie where the good guys beat the bullies. We felt so invincible that we just decided to ramp things up.

We had a fire going on the point, and again, everyone was still pretty inebriated. And my cousin decided to pour a cup full of gasoline on the fire to see how high it would go. You could see what was probably about to happen. We knew it was going to explode, but no one thought it was a bad idea. So as he was about to pour a half gallon of gasoline onto the fire, it shoots up into the cup and explodes everywhere. And I have never seen this happen before or since: I looked down and my jacket was on fire, the ground was on fire, the cup was on fire…everything was on fire.

All my friends were so wasted. They thought it was the funniest thing they ever saw in their lives. Immediately, I sobered up really quick and tried to put it out. I ran down to the lake, grabbed handfuls of water, but nothing worked. I saw my cousin, and he disappeared and ran away. My cousin who started the explosion just ran away. And it wasn't like I could call the fire department. We were on an island-and one filled with dry grass and trees. And I thought, We're going to set this entire island on fire if we are not careful. There was no water system. There was nothing to put it out. And it was getting bigger and bigger and bigger. The other kids are laughing, but I was freaking out… what were we going to do?

Then, out of nowhere, like an angel, my cousin showed up with a fire extinguisher and just managed to put the whole thing out.

We never got caught. No one ever questioned the burn marks on the ground, or my brand-new, cardigan Bugle Boy jacket that was burnt to a crisp. We just woke up the next morning with hangovers and just laughed about it.

This was really indicative of where my life was heading, because it was like the first time in my life I had everything I wanted. I had a new identity that was completely fake. I was living a lifestyle that was completely fake. I was turning my back on friends that had been there since I was five to be something I wasn't. I was slowly spinning out of control. I came back the next summer and crushes turned into romance, and I started living the summer fantasy life I had always dreamed of.

That was when God met me. That was when Christ met me, during my moment of having everything. The girl I liked for all those years was finally mine, and like any smart 9th grader we began to plan out our future together (wedding, kids, jobs etc… you know the normal stuff 14 year olds think about). The parties that I wanted were all reality. The hip-hop I loved was a part of my life. And that same cousin who had nearly set the island on fire had an important conversation with me. He asked, "What's the most important thing in your life? Whatever you say is the most important thing, that's your idol. If you're going to die tomorrow, where are you going? Where are you going to go?"

It was a chilling conversation because it stopped me in that moment. It made me have to decide what was really important.

I took his Bible, woke up the next morning, and started reading the book of Revelation. I read through the entire book in one sitting in the King James version, which is very difficult to understand. It was that pivotal summer of going into my sophomore year that began the process that eventually led to me surrendering my life to Christ.

Higgins Lake represented so many bad decisions, but all those bad decisions were outweighed by the best decision I ever made, which was to surrender my life to Christ.

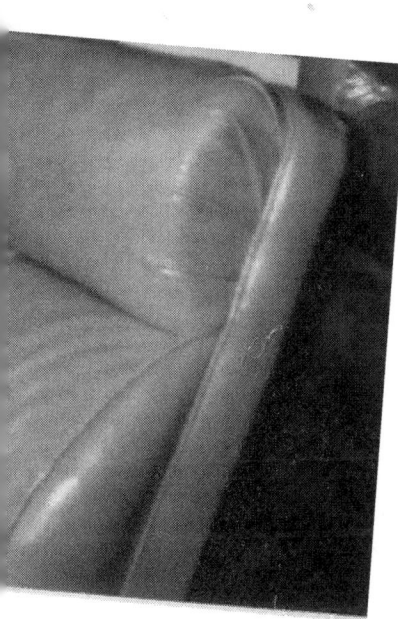

THIS IS LITTERALLY TAKEN THE MORNING AFTER

"one love one God one way..."

CHAPTER 5
THE G-FORCE POSSE

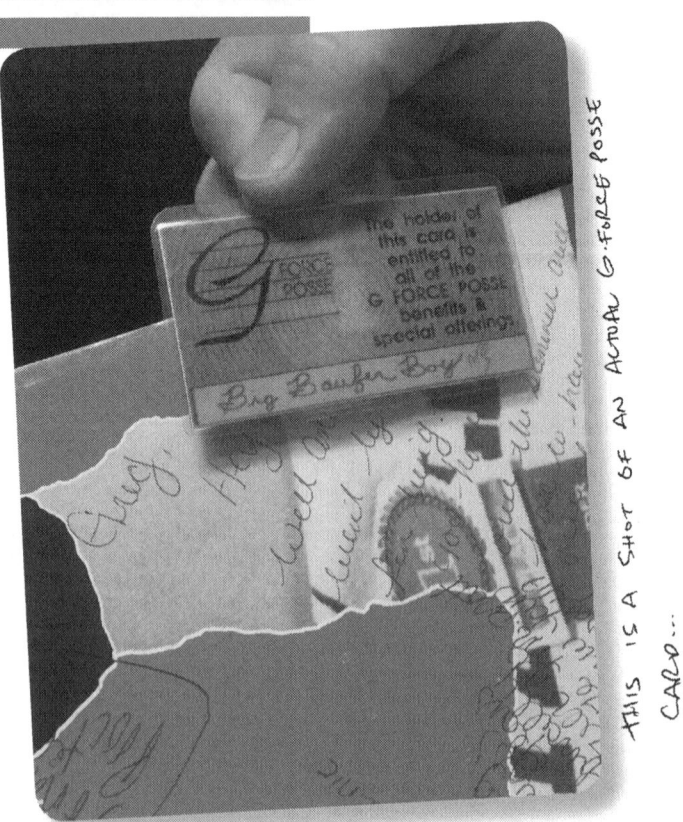

"It is amazing to consider that it all started in my bedroom with a Tascam 4-track cassette recorder and an Ensoniq synth." ~Chris Maconi
(the guy who's room we took over)

Soundtrack to this chapter: "Welcome to the Terrordome" Public Enemy

When I was in eighth grade. I had this friend named Greg. The way I met him was kind of strange. At the time I had a habit of doodling on my desk in one of my classes when I was bored. And I would notice when I would come back the next day, someone had changed my drawings around. After this happened a few times, I realized I and this person-whoever they were-had become a pen pal of sorts, though we had never met face to face. Finally, we ended up meeting and struck up friendship because it turned out we had a ton in common, especially hip-hop music. Due in no small part to our friendship, I started delving deeper into the culture of rap, especially when we entered our freshmen year of high school at Tarpon Springs.

It was always drawing hiphop dudes in Jr. High / High school...

Up to that point I had only listened to party rap...Rob base and DJ EZ Rock, MC hammer, and the like. You have to understand, as a broke ninth-grader, like so many of my peers, I relied heavily on my friends to introduce me to new music. Kids would make copies of their tapes and pass them around class. This was the primary means for sharing music. One day, early in ninth grade, I'll never forget sitting in Spanish class with Greg, which was when he introduced me to a group called Public Enemy. I felt like a whole new universe opened up to me when he showed me their jams, their world. I wanted to learn more, not just about PE, but all things hip hop.

This coincided with the first time my family subscribed to cable TV. Instantly, I felt like so many of my classmates, other teens whose lives were shaped through their connection to pop culture, especially MTV. Immediately, out of my love for hip-hop, Yo! MTV raps became mandatory programming at my house. I watched this show every day after school, as well as on Saturdays. The ritual of tuning in to Fab Five Freddy became like a religion for me. This changed my world, as hip hop was confined to my headphones and speakers prior to that. Because of the visual element of the show, the culture became more real to me, instead of just a mythical unicorn that was far away, in another land (mostly, New York City). The world of my favorite artists felt somehow closer, more realistic. I became a sponge. I was enrolled in rap school 101, constantly yearning for more, determined to become a straight-A student.

Greg dubbed Public Enemy's Yo! Bum Rush the show and It Takes a Nation of Millions to Hold us Back for me. Looking back, these were seminal, foundational records in my career and in my foundation as a human being. I mean these records were, important. I bought into more than just the music, but also the message. The irony in this should be obvious. Greg and I were white kids, yet were way more into hip hop than probably any of the other kids in our classroom, even the black kids. And not just MC Hammer, but militant, black hip-hop. I remember one friend of mine I talked hip-hop with, who was African American, was only into the party, pop artists. I was struck by the fact that I identified more with groups like Public Enemy than he did, because they spoke directly to his experience much more than it did to mine. I actually found myself having to defend the ideology of PE and groups like them to him on more than one occasion.

He thought I was a kook. Can you imagine? This should tell you how deeply the culture of hip-hop, the real-life story of rap resonated with me.

The moment I felt like Greg and I reached our apex of unity in regards to our hip-hop consciousness was when Public Enemy dropped Fear of a Black Planet. The year was 1990. The climate of the time, combined with the music and the message, just hooked me. That was when hip-hop became more than something I listened to. It became something I lived. It was boiling over inside of me, to the point where I had to participate in some way, shape, or fashion. I was super intimidated to become a rapper, so I thought…well, being a DJ would be way more acceptable for a white guy.

Soon, Greg and I were writing really ridiculous raps in his bedroom. It became a means to project an alternate persona; we were embodying everything we wished we were, even if it wasn't reality. The further we went and the more we experimented, the more we began to think we should take it a little more seriously. There was another kid in our class that had also tried his hand at rapping, and "released" a demo tape. Notice the word "released" is in quotes, as his effort was truly less than inspired. He had taken songs by popular artists and he just put his own rhymes on top of pre-existing tracks. I should probably mention he was white as well. We viewed him as illegitimate. So, the actual impetus for starting our "career" was really just a reaction to this kid and his tape. We wanted to prove that we were the real deal, and that he wasn't.

I WAS KILLING IT W/ THE AVIA, MONGOOSE, BOOK BAG + A GAP SWEATSHIRT.

The funny thing about hip-hop is, in a lot of ways, it allows you to speak things into existence before they are even a reality. Many of the rappers I looked up to rocked gold chains. They projected an image of affluence and success, even if it wasn't actually true. It was a dream that you basically faked in the hopes that you would make it for real. So we did the exact same thing.

So we became G-Force Posse.
G.
Force.
Posse.

My friend Greg's name became "Pigz" and mine was "DJ Bones." Our crew was named "G-Force Posse" based on an old cartoon that we grew up watching. As soon as we settled on the names, we began spreading the word to our friends. The response was not overwhelming support, as you can imagine. We became a bit of a joke, as most of our friends couldn't believe we were taking this thing seriously. Every time we told someone about our group, they said, YOU guys don't have a real rap group. That's impossible.

At the time, Greg had a friend that had worked at one of the local music stores at the mall. Remember, this is the late eighties/early nineties, so the mall was everything. It was our hub, so to speak. It was where we bought music, it was where we saw movies, where we met our peers and hung out, and it was the place we tried to meet girls.

Everyone hung out there. So, when Greg convinced his friend to make a fake slot in the hip-hop section for our group, it was a big deal. And because we had no music to fill the G-Force Posse slot on the shelf, it appeared our record was always sold out. So, anytime someone called us out and didn't believe we were legit, we would respond with yo, just go check the shelf at the record store in the mall.

It worked. All we had to do was convince a few kids to visit the record store, and the word spread. We created a persona that was completely illegitimate, yet was totally gaining traction with our peers.

The next step in our "career" was a genius move, or so we thought at the time. It actually was an amazing scheme, and I can't even remember how we came up with it. We thought, let's CHARGE MONEY for our friends to be in the group. In exchange for a few bucks, we would give members a rap name and a membership card to be in the G-Force Posse. Obviously, this was ridiculous. But in a strange way, we were actually inventing a crowdfund campaign. Of course, crowdfunding in the current culture is the financing of creative endeavors through monetizing your most vigilant supporters. You are exchanging music, merch, and the like for an investment on the front end of the endeavor. It's based on the close relationship you have with your most diehard supporters.

So, in 1989, we crowdfunded a nonexistent rap group.

Instead of investing the funds we had coerced from our friends back into the GForce Posse, we took the cash and used it to eat very well at pep rallies and purchased extra snacks at lunchtime. But at some point, we thought, we should probably actually try and do this thing.

That thought led me to another friend's house, a guy named Chris. He had a small recording set up, along with a keyboard beat machine. We had written a couple of raps and we headed over there one day, unannounced, and banged on his bedroom window. He let us in and we got to work.

I need to remind you I was a freshman in high school at this time, again. Meaning, I was in the midst of puberty. Meaning, my voice was changing. So there I was trying to lay down some dope rhymes, and my voice was cracking all over the place. I mean it sounded terrible. Still, somehow, we pushed through and finished our first recording. If I could go back and listen to it, I'm sure it would be the worst thing I have ever heard in my life, but the point is, somehow, we did it.

Now, one thing of note from this "recording session" was the fact that Chris's mom was in the house while we were making music history. And this was before I became a Christian. So I was dropping f-bombs and the like at 100 decibels. At that time I had nothing in my life influencing me to do anything different. But the funny thing about it, looking back, is I can clearly see that God was stirring in my heart, even as I was dropping R-Rated rhymes.

I remember Chris's mom pulled us aside as soon as we were finished recording because she had heard us dropping curses through the door. She said, "Hey, why don't you guys rap about something positive? You could even write Christian rap."

I'll never forget when she hit me with that. I just shook my head and thought, what are you talking about? I didn't even have a response. I didn't say anything to her face, but I thought the idea was absurd. I was so angry because that flew in the face of everything I had convinced myself I was about. I just remember just letting loose a volley of angry profanity to Greg as we walked back to his house. I was defensive because, again, even all the way back then, something spiritual was happening inside of me, even if I wasn't totally aware of it yet.

It's amazing how the things we do in our childhood set the stage for our future, and how seemingly insignificant decisions and relationships come back around. Fast forward twenty years. Chris, without whom I would have never made that first recording, became one of my largest contributors to my first crowdfunded albums after I left the major label system. To this day he still stands as one of the largest financial supporters I have had to date.

As it turns out, when I was able to reconnect with him through my music career, I had the opportunity to set things right with both him and his mom for my angry outburst all those years prior. I apologized to them both, even if neither he nor his mom heard the words I had said behind her back. The fact was, the words of his mom, even in the midst of my teenage rebellion, played a role in the person I later became.

Amazingly enough, years later, I had the opportunity to speak at the exact same church his family had attended since back in the day when we made that tape. I was able to share this story, and about the principle of sowing seeds in the lives of others.

You just never know when your words will take root in the life of someone else.

CHAPTER 6
I ALMOST BECAME A MORMON

MY FRIENDS CIRCLE LOOKED LIKE A BENNETON CLOTHING AD...

"Do you love the Bible? We have the accompaniment to the Bible..."
Mormon commercial 1990

Soundtrack to this chapter: "Run for Cover" Dynamic Twins

I gave my life to Jesus when I was fifteen. Just before that, I was going through a very deep time of "searching." During that time, I watched a lot of TBN, listened to several Christian radio shows, and read my little brother's children's picture Bible. So I had this very limited perception of God in those days. Before long, I began thinking, I should probably get my hands on a Bible. But, I was fifteen and broke as a joke. And it wasn't like anyone was going to just walk up to me and hand me one.

AH GOOD OLD WHITE EGYPTIANS... YIKES...

I remember just sitting there, watching TV, as I was thinking about this. And as I was, a Mormon commercial came on. I felt as if the voice on the tube was speaking directly to me:

"Do you believe in the Bible?" The Mormon commercial said to me.
I said (out loud), "Yeah, I do."

"Well, we have the accompaniment to the Bible, called The Book of Mormon. We have an 800 number, and you can give us a call! We will send you The Book of Mormon free of charge!"

So I thought to myself, problem solved; until I get a Bible, I'll get this Book of Mormon. So, a couple of days later it arrived and I started reading it. I mean, I really started reading it, like, faithfully, because, in my head, God was really working in my life at that moment. After all, he had miraculously provided me with the book for free.

I want to be clear: though I was completely misguided, I really had a genuine desire to figure who God really was. So I took time out of every day to read a couple chapters of the new book I thought He had provided for me. I just started at the beginning. To be blunt, I was completely confused by what I read and I didn't connect with it at all, but I was determined to push through because, I thought, God deserves my best.

I know... amazing, right?

A few days after I began reading, things took a major turn. I came upon a story that described a curse that God made upon the people who didn't migrate to North America from the Middle East. It literally said that the curse was BLACK SKIN. When I read this, I was utterly and completely shocked. I went from confused/bored out of my mind to completely enthralled. I had to keep reading and re-reading the part over and over. I thought, this can't be what I think it is. You're telling me that because this group of people didn't do what God said, that he cursed them and made them black (2 Nephi 5:21-23).

Obviously, I didn't know much about God at the time, or The Book of Mormon, or the Bible for that matter. But even my fifteen-year-old, Biblically illiterate self knew something was totally off. Did God really say all black people are cursed because their ancestors didn't follow His people into North America? I thought hard about it and prayed about it, like, sincerely.

After I did, that was the last day I opened the book of Mormon. I just closed it and put it aside. I thought, I don't know much about God, but that doesn't sound like Him. The God I heard about, that I had given my life to, wouldn't say that skin tone defined your standing with him. I had friends from every possible walk of life, you know? The picture of my graduating class looked like a color wheel. One of my good friends was from South America, and other friend was Puerto Rican, another was black, another was white, and still another was Lebanese. Nearly every single one of my friends was from a different race. With all that was in me I couldn't believe God would associate the color of skin with any sort of judgment.

Right after I had these thoughts, the phone rang. No joke, it was the Mormon church following up with me. They said, "Hey, we know we sent you the book. We're just curious what you think!"

I just said, "No thanks, I'm good," and just hung up the phone.

It took me another couple of months, but I finally got my hands on a real Bible. It was my cousin's, and it was a King James version. I'm not going to lie, it was super hard to understand, because the language was all old English. But I said, you know what, I don't care. I'm going to get to know God. So, I just started reading chapter after chapter, and I devoured it. Within, literally, the first year I had read through the entire thing. I'm not bragging, I am just letting you know how hungry I was.

A couple of months later, I wandered into this tiny little Assemblies of God church by myself. I started attending regularly. My mom would drop me off and pick me up after. And this little church loved on me with such an intense love. I'll be honest with you, the thing that drew me to this church was that when I walked in, it was one third Jamaican, one third Puerto Rican, and one third Caucasian. Everybody was so excited, and I thought, you know what? This is what heaven has to be like.

Right around that time, they actually gave me a VHS tape called The God Makers. It was, basically, an expose' on the Mormon church. I popped it in, and it was a cartoon. I just sat there with my jaw wide open. Soon, I realized how different Mormonism was from what I believed it was.

Fast-forward many years. I am doing my music, and it gains traction on a bunch of Mormon websites, recommended as good, wholesome Christian music. Because of this, along with my rise in popularity, I started amassing a sizeable Mormon following-kids, adults, teens, you name it. At one point, I did an interview with American Bible Society. I shared a story about the validity of the Bible, and why I didn't become a Mormon.

Then, I started getting emails suggesting that I reexamine the book of Mormon. Some of these emails suggested I should pray about it. They said, we're good Christians, too. The thing I realized is that a majority of those that are in the Mormon church don't know most of the wacky things buried in their writings, teachings, and theology. It's very much a religion based on feelings. The reality is, Mormonism is based on progressive revelation, which means over time they can change their stance on what they believe and teach because God's message also can change.

In other words, black people were barred from the priesthood until the 1970's, then all of a sudden God changed His mind.

Look, I still have a sizable Mormon fan base. I still have friends that are in the Mormon church. So this isn't me trying to argue Mormons out of their faith. All I am saying is that in the Book of Acts, they questioned everything and they checked it with the scripture.

And I have done that as well. So, if you're telling me people are cursed because their skin is black, I'm sorry, but that is not the God I serve.

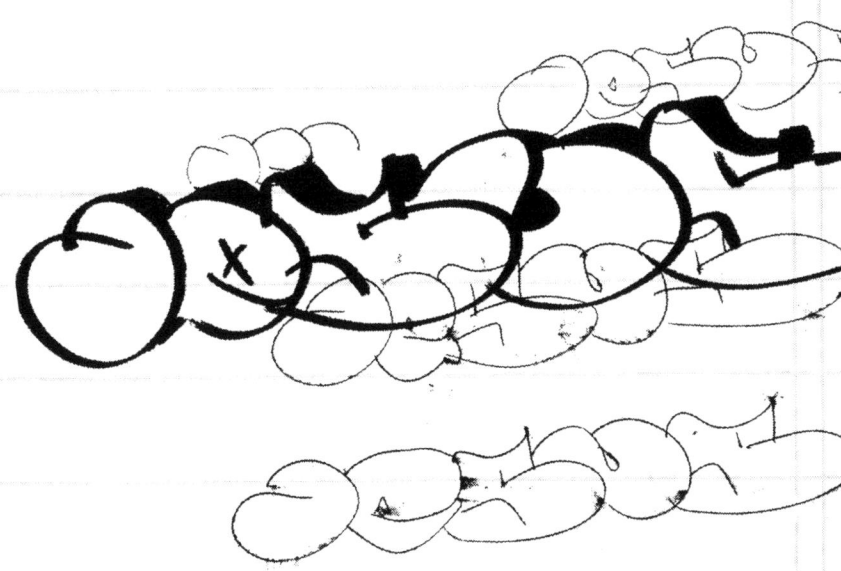

CHAPTER 7
HOW I WROTE MY FIRST RAP

THE 90'S WAS All ABOUT BEADS & AThLETHIC TEAMS YOU DON'T EVEN LIKE.

> "It was pretty scary and I remember him looking kinda nervous. I had a feeling it was gonna be awesome. He explained it a little (I remember him talking about feeling "set free" that weekend), got us clapping a beat, and he started rapping and it was like he'd been doing it all his life." Lyle Baker (who was in the audience for that first rhyme)

Soundtrack for this chapter: "Back From the Grave" by King J-Mack

By my senior year of high school I was a really committed Christian kid. I was on the football team and I was also a member of the track team. It was strange because rap had been completely pushed out of the picture in my life. I mean, I had written raps before I was a believer, but by my last year of high school I was just an excited, young believer who was going on to do ministry. That was all that was really on my horizon….no rapping, no battles, no record deals or tours.

I was about to graduate, and I had what is commonly referred to as "senior-itis." I was over school, and I was completely unmotivated to do much of anything. I just wanted to graduate and get on with the next step, you know? So I decided to become a pole-vaulter my senior year because I had a good friend from church who did it as well. Not coincidentally, he had really turned me on to Christian hip-hop, as well. So because we were homies, I wanted to do what he did…which was very little. Pole-vaulting was an easy way to get a third varsity letter without doing much work, instead of running the half-mile or quarter mile, which I had participated in previously. It was an easy way for me to coast for the last couple of months of school.

THE FLORIDA HUMIDITY WRECKED HAVOC ON MY HAIR… IT ALWAYS POOFED UP IN A MINI FRO.

I found out very quickly that I was a terrible pole-vaulter, but I honestly didn't care. My pole-vaulter friends and I literally sat around all day long. We could have ordered pizza if we wanted to. I felt like it was the perfect situation.

During pre-season, we did this drill where we put the bar up as high as possible. It was set at like twenty-one feet. The whole point of the drill is to lean back as far as you can to kick the bar off; it was meant to teach you to have good pole-vaulting form. So, it was my turn, and I had been horrible up to that point. But, I went for it, anyway, I leaned all the way back, but I completely missed the bar. I flew onto the pole vault pit and the momentum of my back hitting the mat threw my knees into my face. So, my shoulders hit, then my knees hit my face and the force of my knees hitting my face broke my nose. But I didn't realize I broke it at first; I just thought I had a bloody nose. I leaned over the pole vault pit and a water faucet of blood came out of my nose.

I looked at my friend and he just recoiled in horror. I reached up and I realized my nose was half way on the side of my face. So they ushered me off to the clinic. I had to get surgery, and the season was over before I made it back. To this day I still have a bump on my nose because it never healed correctly, and it probably changed the tone of my voice. The byproduct of the whole thing was I got stuck at home. I had a cast on my nose that looked like a gigantic Oxy pad. I couldn't go back to school because I had to heal.

So, a couple days into this I was bored out of mind. I had an instrumental side of a record to an old 3rd Bass song and I just said, you know what? I'm going to write my story in a rap form.

Boredom was the true stimulus for my first rap.

I started writing and it was pretty cool. I figured I would show my friends some day, but never did I think I would become a rapper.

About a month later, I am about to graduate. I still couldn't run track or pole-vault. I really didn't know what I was going to do after high school. Then, I went to this camp where God just did a major work in my life. I had been holding onto tons of bitterness, hurt, and pain, and God took the whole weight of that in one night. After that night, I went to this thing called an afterglow. It was basically a talent show, and opportunity to showcase something you were interested in or had a knack for doing. Everyone cheered each other on. I realized the only thing I really had that I could do was this rap I had memorized.

So, I was outside the camp and I was pacing, totally nervous. I was freaking out because I didn't even have a beat. What was I going to do? So, I said, forget it. Who Cares?

So, I walked back in and I told the crowd to start clapping their hands to make a beat. And I rapped to the hand clap beat, but I quickly realized I had never written a chorus to my rap. The only thing I could come up with was, throw your hands in the air waving like you just don't care. It was a great idea, except it eliminated all the clapping. So, I just destroyed the whole song before I even started.

This was how my rap career was born.

Everyone ran up to me with their minds blown. Everyone said, dude, I never knew you could do that. I had to acknowledge the power that hip-hop had to get people's attention.

I thought about it, and decided to write a few more raps. Right after graduation I decided to go in to a legitimate studio to record them, for no other reason than to just say I did it. And if anything has ever defined my career, it's not that I've been the most talented, but that I was always willing to try and fail.

Where other people would have let fear stop them, I believed that God was big enough to provide. I also believed God was big enough that if I missed the mark He would put me back on track.

I went in the studio and recorded my first four-song demo. My rap name was King J Mack. The album was titled Back from the grave, and it was terrible, of course. But it was a starting point, and the reason I came to call myself KJ52.

I DONT EVEN KNOW WHAT TO SAY ABOUT THIS PIC... I WAS SO NOT THUGGISH... WEARING A SKULLY + SWEATSHIRT IN FLORIDA MAKES O SENSE.

I realized I wasn't the most talented, I didn't have a lot to offer, but just like the five loaves and two fish, I gave Christ whatever I had.

Here I am all these years later, and he has multiplied it. And it all started with a broken nose.

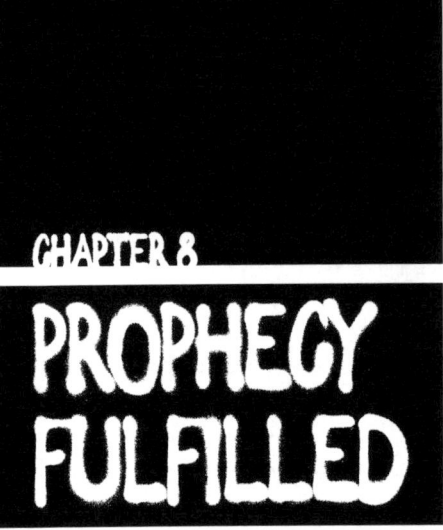

CHAPTER 8
PROPHECY FULFILLED

THIS WAS THE ACTUAL ARTICLE THEY PRINTED

"I don't walk like an emcee but i flow.." King J-Mack

Soundtrack for this chapter: "I don't" by King J-Mack

42 | What Happened Was...

I would consider myself to be a charismatic with a seatbelt. Meaning, I do believe that God still does miracles. I still believe in what is called the gifts of the Spirit. But, I am also not what I would call a "Charismaniac." So, I don't believe in complete unabashed craziness when it comes to prophecies or the like. I believe in testing experience with the scriptures. The Bible says if a prophecy comes true then that person was a real prophet. And if it doesn't you should probably grab stones and hit them…I kid, of course. I've always been pretty hesitant about ascribing God's name to an apparent manifestation of His Spirit, if that makes sense. I guess the best way to describe my belief would be cautiously optimistic.

But in the early days of my charismatic journey, in the early to mid-nineties, it was a different story.

One of my very early shows in my career was a fly date, meaning I took a plane to the performance. There, I opened for an early pioneering Christian Hip hop group called Gospel Gangstaz. At the time, I idolized those guys. I thought they were amazing, so the chance to meet them was exciting. I mean, they were (at one point) real gang bangers, the real deal. It was just a moment when I truly had a chance to meet my heroes. Remember, though, that this was a long time ago. I was literally still a kid, all of about nineteen years old.

I remember right before I went on stage they just treated me with so much love and acceptance, even though I wasn't very good at my craft yet. They prayed with me for fifteen minutes or so, and I was super pumped. But right after that, just as I was about to walk onstage, their manager stopped me and started talking to me. He said, "God's going to bring the woman you're going to marry into your life when you come back from this show."

So, after the show, of course, I am looking everywhere for the girl back home in my town. For the next few days and even weeks I am leaving no stone unturned, but she is not showing up. I even went on a few dates shortly thereafter, thinking each time she was going to be my wife. But none of those girls were the right fit for me. I thought, where is she? Of course, I had believed his "prophecy," so I was completely beside myself as to why I couldn't find "the one." A couple months later I was getting ready to go off to Bible college and I thought, Yeah, that's it. I'm going to meet the woman I'm going to marry at school…

So, this idea was set in my mind, and I resolved that this prophecy was going to come to fruition when I went away. But a few weeks before I left I went on a date with the woman who would become my wife. This is where the story becomes crazy, though. Unbeknownst to me, her mom (now, my mother in-law) had seen an article about me in the local paper before we ever met. Understand, I had never met my wife or her mom yet. Her mom told me later that when she read the article she had a feeling in her spirit that her daughter was going to marry me. She didn't share this until a couple of years later.

I THINK WE PAID $45 FOR THIS TREE, THAT WAS PROBABLY ALL WE HAD.

Christmas 98 "Our First Christmas"

Again, I think the best way to evaluate a "prophecy" is to simply see if it comes true. I realize there are many cases of self-fulfilled prophecies, but in this case, it was just too crazy to write-off. The reality is that when I met my wife I was not looking at her as a potential mate, because I was resolved that my future lady was waiting for me at Bible College. I was thinking I was just going to go on one date. I was being extra cautious. I even invited her to go to the housing projects to do kids ministry in one of the roughest spots in Ft Myers, Florida-you know, to put her through an extra layer of fire. But looking back, now, it's hard to say anything but that God wasn't all over the situation.

Another situation regarding prophetic words happened to me right around the same time. I performed this tiny little show in a hotel lobby in Sarasota at this over-the-top charismatic church that met there. They had me in to rap on a Sunday morning, even though I was far from being on a professional level yet. Again, this was early in my career, so I was long on passion, but very short on skill. I had only been rapping for a couple of months, so there was nothing indicating that I had any sort of prodigious ability. Nevertheless, the people at the church were so nice and hospitable to me that I couldn't help but see Jesus in them.

The pastor's wife spoke to me during the middle of the service. She stopped everything to share something with me. She said, "God wants you to know, to wait on his timing. Some day, He's going to bring you in front of kings and senators and powerful people. You're going to share your gift all across the world."

I remember thinking, OK lady, I'm just going to tuck this away. We'll see if this one ever comes true. I had my doubts, of course. Fast forward ten years ahead, and I am in Texas. George W. Bush had just stepped down as president. And I am performing right before he speaks at the Get Motivated Seminar at his first speaking event after his presidency. There was secret service, and thousands upon thousands in attendance.

I couldn't write a script like this, even if I was trying to. It's impossible to deny there was something legitimate, something divine to what the lady so many years ago had said to me.

I actually opened up for an actual, U.S. president, and previously, before senators and one of the Kings of Morocco. The Get Motivated Seminars had some really high end, important people, and I performed at those events many times.

I remember going to the other side of the stadium and just reflecting on all of it for a few minutes. And just then I realized what she had said had become true.

CHAPTER 9
GUN SHOTS ON MLK

GOLDIN CHILD IS BEING SWALLOWED BY HIS JACKET...

"No matter your opinion on KJ's methods in ministry, there is no denying the evident effectiveness of his ministry. Since I've known him his discipleship to faith in Jesus has helped me shape my walk with Christ" ~ Jack Marlowe aka Goldinchild

Soundtrack to this chapter: "Itsoweezee" De La Soul
(we were freestyling to the instrumental when all this happpened)

Around 1996, I started working at this inner city church. During my tenure there it was the first place my wife and I had ever gone on a date. At that time, I basically stopped playing around and I said, the girl that I'm going to marry, she has to at least be able to go to the hood with me and do ministry to kids on a Saturday. And she agreed.

Fast forward a year or two later, and the same church hired me on as a ministry coordinator. One thing you have to understand is at the time that neighborhood was labeled one of the most segregated cities in the south by an independent study. The church was located in this tiny little section of Ft. Myers, Florida called Dunbar. It was actually on the map because so many phenomenal athletes had come out of the area. Javon Kearse's nephew was in my youth group. Deion Sanders' childhood house was down the street. If you've ever heard of the rapper named Plies, before he was a famous rapper, I used to play him in football. So, this small community had a lot of history.

Due to all the racial undertones, I constantly found myself in hot water. Once I tried to engage with The Nation of Islam guys selling bean pies and the Final Call newspaper. They basically thought I was a cop so they really wouldn't converse with me. Another time, there was a guy down the street who used to sell velvet paintings of Jesus. He was an orthodox Muslim, but he was black. He told me he became a Muslim because of all the racist Christians he had to deal with in the military. Another time there was a slightly mentally deranged guy that I think was using The Nation of Islam to feed his hatred of white people. So, when I was onstage at the church, he'd be in the middle of the audience clutching his Koran, standing up while everybody else sat down, just trying to stare me down. If push came to shove, he would have probably started swinging at me. All of this was swirling around me as I went to work at this church.

At the time, my hip-hop career was just gaining legs. I hadn't gotten a deal yet, though. And if anything, I thought, Oh, now that I'm on staff at a church, I pretty much have to give up on my rap dreams. But God seemed to be constantly bringing it back into focus. I felt like He kept telling me that He gave me the talent and passion to rap for a reason. So, I would rap for my kids or I would go out into the projects to freestyle. I think that's how I became decent at freestyle, because I was constantly being put on the spot during that time. People would always test me and put me on the spot like "rap… whiteboy." So you have to understand I had to be a little bit better than average just to be able to hang. All of this contributed to my identity as it is now.

THIS WAS THE ACTUAL STAGE/SETUP WHERE IT ALL HAPPENED…

One story I never will forget happened when I just started working at that church, in the very first month I was there. I have to mention that the place was located on Martin Luther King Boulevard. So, every Sunday night there were massive parties being thrown by the liquor store across the street, and people would park their cars all up and down the way. We were right across the street from all this, and the neighborhood was absolute pandemonium.

I have to tell you, the church was actually started by a white lady from Dallas who just went into the projects to reach kids. It began to grow and grow until it became an actual church. She was a super feisty and fearless woman. So, she organized a group of us to evangelize on a Sunday night, right there in the midst of all the insanity. We had these gigantic trucks that would fold down on the side and create a stage. We had a sound system set up. And she told me I was going to rap, she was going to preach, and all the rowdy folks were either going to get off the property or get saved.

In hindsight, this plan was actually kind of dangerous. I couldn't drive down the street without drug dealers blocking in my car or pounding on my door. It was a high crime area. So, I was standing out there with my then girlfriend and my former rhyme partner Goldin Child, who was still a teenager at the time. It was late. There were cars everywhere. Music was blasting. Church Pastor Lady is onstage just preaching her guts out. She was telling everyone in earshot if they continued in their lifestyle, it would only end one of two ways…in jail, or dead. I mean, she wasn't being condemning, she was just being honest. She basically asked the neighborhood why not surrender your life to Jesus? It was actually a very inviting message. And after she spoke she handed me the mic and just told me to start rapping.

Remember, this was in the very early stages of my hip-hop endeavors. I didn't even have enough songs to fill the time. I just played beats and started freestyling with Goldin Child. And I really wasn't getting through to anybody. No one was paying attention. Cars were just continuing to drive by.

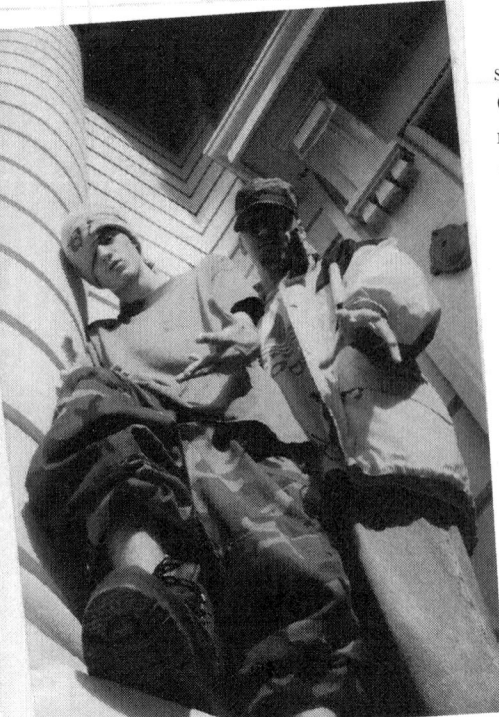

1990's pics were all about hands coming at ya! LOL! RAWR!

And I'll never forget this: Clear as day, as I'm sitting there rhyming, I see this guy driving slow. Out comes his arm…And I see the gun…He was maybe ten feet away from me. He points it straight up in the air and…

POW, POW, POW!

It was like firecrackers.

You would think in that moment I would have panicked. You would think I would have freaked out and ran. Instead, I just incorporated it into my freestyle. I rapped ambulance sirens.. gun shots firing. I was just reacting to what was happening in the moment without freaking. And though everyone ducked for a moment, no one else ran either. Then, awesome, bold church founder lady asked me for the mic. So, I give it to her, and as I did the guy in the car turned around. He started driving back the opposite direction, toward us, to make another pass. Then, he pulled the gun out in the middle of her preaching and fired again!

The whole vibe changed the second time around. Everyone knew the dude was serious. Instead of staying put, she stage dove behind a speaker. Everybody started running. My wife, (then girlfriend) just stood there, though, and froze. So, I grabbed her and Goldin Child, and I went behind the stage to find cover.

After the second shots were fired it was time to pack it up.
Party's over. Time to go.

I remember thinking about how close I came to losing my life. I still think about it. That was literally within the first three weeks of being on the job. I look back in a lot of ways and think it was those forces of darkness in the neighborhood who inspired the shots. It was as if the enemy was saying, oh, you think you can just set up a stage here and wreck shop, do you? But I took it as a challenge, and I think God gave me the strength to become even more determined to stay the course after that scary night.

The experience taught me so much about staying true to your calling, and to never give up no matter what happens.

CHAPTER 10
BOOED OFF THE STAGE AT TRIBE CALLED QUEST

THATS LITTERALLY A YOUTH GROUP T-SHIRT ON GOLDIN CHILDS HEAD...

"I'll battle anyone who comes on this stage! Yall don't know real hip hop!"
~ Goldinchild 1996

Soundtrack to this chapter: "Worldwide" Sons of Intellect

Right around the time that Goldin Child and I had started a group, we felt a real passion to be a light in the darkness. This was the early days of the internet. So, I would go to my local public library, hop on the Internet, and research concerts that were coming to Florida. I looked for mainstream artists, primarily. When I found a show I thought I would be good fit for us, I would start hitting up the promoters. I found shows all over Florida–from Orlando to Miami, to South beach to my local neighborhood to Tampa. Our philosophy was to simply be as dope as possible with our show, and then maybe we would get a chance to share our faith offstage.

It was very much a matter of earning respect first in that world. Only after you earned a measure of it could you share what you believe. We had been heavily influenced by a few rappers who had that sort of approach and methodology. Our only problem was the fact that we were two white guys. I know, obvious, right? But, it was a factor that no one thought about. Florida was so segregated, and so racially divided at the time, there were times we wouldn't get a chance to even perform because we would just immediately get booed. It was tough, man. But after trying to slug it out for a bit as a local opener to mainstream groups, we heard about a pivotal opportunity.

A Tribe Called Quest was coming through, and I was in touch with the promoter. He put us on the bill as one of four openers.

So, we roll in to the show and the whole thing is running late. This is a mainstream hip-hop thing, for sure-shows are always late, especially ones with well-known artists. So, they pushed back our set by several hours. The crowd just sat there for what seemed like forever. Of course, they were becoming increasingly agitated.

So then, we had an idea. We wanted to go on stage and incorporate a creative beat box into the songs. I had a friend who was there hanging out and he warned us not do it. He said the crowd wouldn't go for it. I was all for it, because it had killed at other shows at the time.

The crowd tolerated us for the first couple of songs, but by the third song they were starting to become restless. Then, they literally started picking up stuff and just throwing it at us in massive amounts. A few started booing, then the boos spread to the rest of the crowd. I don't know if you have ever experienced 800 people booing you, but there aren't many things worse. At that point, I felt like we needed to cut our losses. But, Goldin Child was the scrappiest sixteen-year-old around. He basically said, I'll battle anybody to come on this stage right now. That's when the crowd transformed into a mass of potential murderers. The room became a frenzy of anger, directed solely at us. I may or may not have shouted "Jesus is Lord" or something to the that effect as I grabbed Goldin Child and we fled for our lives to the backstage.

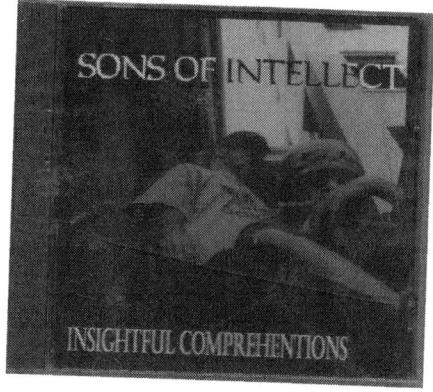

ONLY GOT LIKE TWO COPIES LEFT

In hindsight, I realized my philosophy was completely off, because the reality was I was never going to get past the hurdle that was already in people's minds...I was a white guy doing hip-hop.

Around that time, I had a conversation at the time with Ambassador from Cross movement. I told him about our dilemma, and he basically said, better that they boo you for being a Christian rather than boo you for being a white guy. But, I was so discouraged. I wanted to give up on the mainstream shows. I had basically threw in the towel, when a couple of days later, a promoter called me and asked if we wanted to open for De La Soul in Ybor city. It was unbelievably significant because I loved De La Soul growing up, and the show was two blocks from where I used to live.

I was super nervous because I basically had PTSD after the Tribe fiasco. I went into it prepared to get booed off the stage again.

I decided to alter my approach. I was going to let people know, up front-not in a preachy way-what we stand for. I took the advice of Ambassador. So, I told the crowd we were believers in Christ and that our music was influenced by our faith right when we took the stage. No one booed. They sat through our songs and we made it through the set all in one piece.

It definitely made me realize that there is power in Jesus' name. Likewise, there is no power in my own name. I have nothing to offer in and of myself. So it shifted the whole philosophy.

Within a year my group with Goldin Child broke up. So, once I was not in a group anymore, I started to get more creative with how I shared my light in the darkness. One night, I went to an open mic with cassettes that had my music with a gospel presentation on them. I gave them away like I would give away a gospel tract. What I didn't consider was the fact that those things made great missiles...They all came flying back at me when I performed. I literally was dodging my own music being chucked at my head. Then, five guys in the front row of the show put their middle fingers right in my face, as they were throwing the cassette projectiles, as well. The boo's started flowing in the crowd, and I thought...man, here we go again.

All of these experiences taught me you just have to shrug the losses off and keep it moving.

All of this led to one of the bigger shows that I ended up doing about a year later. At the time, I had my first record deal, but I didn't have an album out yet. Vanilla ice came out to play at the same club where I opened up for De La Soul. I connected with the promoter and he gave me a forty-five minute set.

I had played enough shows at that point that I realized a Vanilla Ice crowd was going to be different than a De La Soul crowd, which was different than a hood club open mic. So, I really put in the work to make sure my show was on point. I had so much drive at that moment because I was in the beginning stages of going solo. I went into that show with a specific strategy. I was very up front with who I was in my faith, and the crowd erupted in applause. I looked out and I realized it was a completely different audience. It was mostly skater kids, which is more of a rock-oriented crowd. It went so well that I wound up opening for Vanilla Ice again but this time it was in my hometown.

After so much trial and error with the show and especially the ministry, I finally started to hone in on things. I added my DJ to the show. And we played a run of shows leading up to the hometown Vanilla Ice performance. My live show was really coming together and I wanted to be even more strategic with how I approached that night specifically. So, I printed what appeared to be club flyers, but it was actually an ad for the entrance to "club paradise." So really, it was a gospel tract that looked like a club flyer. And I thought…this is a real easy way for me to share my faith in a club. I could start a conversation by inviting someone to a "special spot," and then I could open up and share about who Christ was.

I remember taking the stage vividly. I told the crowd what I was about, and they started applauding. It was a good start. I started freestyling, and at one point I saw something fly through the air and hit me in the face. I started getting flashbacks, again. I started bracing myself for the boos. I looked down on the ground and it's a WWJD bracelet. This guy in the crowd was so excited that a Christian was on stage, he ripped off his bracelet off and threw it at me.

And honestly, the show was amazing. It's almost sad to say it, but I realized that I was going to be accepted way more readily by a non hip-hop crowd. That show started to make me shift my thinking. I accepted that I was always going to struggle with the white aspect in a rap crowd, even though I went on to do more battles and I continued to learn how to hold my own. It really changed my philosophy in some ways to consider that in one place the ground was hard to plow, but in another it was bearing fruit.

I realized that there was a whole group of kids that loved hip-hop that were not necessarily hip-hop kids. They were struggling and they needed someone to give them some hope. And that thought represented a new shift in my music. And that thought process really built the foundation for my career for the next ten to fifteen years.

CHAPTER 11
THEY PUT ME ON THE GANG FILE

THIS WAS ONE OF THE PICS FROM THE PHOTO SHOOT..

"Freeze... don't move.. put your hands up and back up slowly" FMPD 1998

Soundtrack to play for this chapter: "One Time" Gospel Gangstaz

When I was seven years old, I lived in Ybor City with my dad, which at the time was a very financially depressed part of Tampa, Florida. As far as I remember, I was the only white kid in my entire neighborhood. It's not that there weren't other white folks-there were a few-but they were all adults in their thirties or forties, and these are the artistic types who stood out like sore thumbs. So, to say I was a minority in my own community would be an understatement; I was the only kid who was not Cuban or African American. My best friend (who was Cuban) wasn't even from my neighborhood and was never even allowed to spend the night at my house because his parents were worried about the safety of my hood.

And I do mean "hood."

We lived in an apartment behind my dad's storefront, in the same space. And around this time, break-ins became a regular part of life for us. Usually, this would consist of my dad and I leaving for the afternoon, only to return to have the back door to the store kicked in and the place looted. To attempt to rectify this, my dad would hire various people from the community to sweep up and do odd jobs. The thinking was that if people from the neighborhood were employed there, by association everyone else would stop targeting us. I remember one guy he hired was named "Killer." The name alone should have been a fair warning to us, but my dad was so desperate to stop the rampant ransacking that he was willing to give almost anyone a shot. Well, Killer ended up casing the place, and though we could never prove it, we think he was one of the many people who ended up robbing us.

AN ARTICLE THEY PUBLISHED ON MY DAD & HIS STUDIO...

A particular memory sticks out in mind which represents this chapter in our lives. One night, my dad woke up and caught someone coming through the window of the shop. He screamed at the guy, and the would-be robber was so scared he screamed back, then fell backwards out of the window. Luckily, I was a heavy sleeper and didn't witness any of this first hand.

I only mention all of this to paint the picture that there were a lot of things working against us in the neighborhood. My dad's plan to hire neighborhood folks to befriend them failed to deter robberies. So, he had to go another route. He wasn't the type to own a gun, even though he would have been completely justified in doing so. He just wasn't into firearms, and in fact, I had never even shot a gun my entire life up until just a couple of years ago.

So because guns were off the table, he decided to get a dog instead. Only, he didn't just buy a Labrador or a Collie. He wanted a menacing animal who would sit in the doorway of the shop and really deter people who might have been thinking of ripping us off.

I'll never forget the day the dog fairy showed up at our studio. And I mean this literally-one of my dad's friends dressed up like an actual fairy to deliver our new pooch/monster. Can you imagine? Our neighborhood was composed of some characters, to say the least. This lady was committed to the costume and the character. When she came in she said, I'm the dog fairy and I'm here to grant you your wishes. She produced this crossbred German Shepherd-esque pup. He was basically a mutt with several different breeds running through him, but I guess he resembled a Shepherd the most. I remember he was tall. He grew up to be a very, big dog, and he had gigantic ears.

I need to remind you this was the eighties. And I was a kid who was obsessed with sci-fi. So, when my dad gave me permission to name the dog, naturally only one name came to mind:

Tron.

I loved (and still love) that movie. Don't get me wrong, he ended up becoming a great dog, all things considered. Really, my only memory of him acting out was when, every once in a while, he escaped off his leash and ran to the fish market next door. He would sneak in the back and roll around in the fish guts, then return to us reeking, drenched in chum.

Tron did have one distinctive, "unique" personality trait, however. We were in a high foot-traffic area, next to a parking lot and on the main drag next to all the shops and businesses. My dad would chain him up inside the store so his leash would only reach to the doorway and no further. Again, people of various ethnicities and backgrounds walked by the front of the shop all day, day in and day out. Most of the day, Tron just hung out inside of the store. But, you have to picture this: A white dude would walk by, and the dog would just sit there in the store. A Cuban guy would walk by, and the dog would just sit there. Puerto Rican guy would walk by, and the dog wouldn't pay him any mind...

THIS IS THE DOOR HE USED TO COME CHARGING OUT OF..

But when a black guy would walk by, the dog would lose it's mind…roaring and snarling and galloping toward the door at top speed until the chain would yank him back, with fantastic, cartoonish violence, just as he hit the door way. And every time he did this, the guy he was going after would jump back absolutely terrified. Each and every "victim" would jump ten paces into the middle of the street, while Tron would just bark bloody murder for about a minute. Then, the dog would chill out and calmly strut back to the middle of the store to lay down again.

This would happen over and over again. So after a certain point, we had to ask ourselves…

Was Tron a racist dog?

It was kind of hard to ignore the facts: brown, brown, brown, white… nothing.

Then, every single time a black man strolled by…

BWAAAARRRAAAORRRAAARRGGGH!!!

It certainly wasn't like we were sicking him on anyone ever, especially not a specific race. Do you understand? We never did one single thing to instill this in him. And it was only African Americans he went after.

I guess that was the first time in my life that I became aware of racism as an actual thing in the world, strangely enough. I realized that people formulate opinions based on nothing more than the appearance of skin. And indirectly, because of that dog, my dad really did use the situation as an opportunity to teach me that all people have value. I learned you can't formulate a response about people based on the way they appear; each person is a unique individual with a colorless soul, so to speak. This was years before I became a Christian. I knew racism was wrong, I knew that my dog was wrong.

Ironically, right around the same time, I was attending a private, Catholic school and, I'll never forget it, to this day-they actually played a song that was titled "What Color is God's Skin?" I remember all of this very clearly; we sat down in the class and the teacher would play the song…What color is God's skin? Is it black, Brown, or yellow? Is it red? Is it white? Everyone's the same in the good Lord's sight.

Diversity… uniqueness... race. At age seven, I understood everyone is the same… and this was and is a beautiful thing.

In no small part due to Tron, the racist dog.

CHAPTER 4
I ALMOST BURNED THE ISLAND DOWN

NOT GONNA LIE THIS WAS A SWEET BODY GLOVE T-SHIRT I HAD ON..

"It has hurt my heart to know that such a dear friend experienced such intense hurt during what we all know are notoriously difficult developmental years. I had very little idea what social mayhem was going on behind the scenes, nor did I realize the internal struggle. In the simplest, most pure form, I just knew that I cared so much. I could only hope that by unlocking the natural gifts and talents he has always possessed, that someday things would turn around for Jonah. The island in so many ways represents generations of life experience and family. It is and always will be a precious adventure that embraces and binds those who adventure with her." ~ Amy (the girl in the story)

Soundtrack to this chapter: "Never Tear Us Apart" by INXS

Right around the time when I was working at Cornerstone Church, I was close to releasing my debut solo album. At this point the group I was in with Goldin Child had phased out. I was really just beginning to focus on my solo career. It was a new, interesting creative time for me because, for the first time, I had a really clear understanding of what I wanted to do artistically, but I wasn't part of a group anymore.

Goldin Child's younger brother was a photographer, and he was just kind of starting out, as well. So, I recruited him to take pictures for my first solo photo shoot. The shoot was as low budget of a situation as could be. I explained to him that I make $7.50 an hour as a youth pastor at this little hood church down the street. Because he was not yet established either, he agreed.

We began shooting in downtown Fort Myers. I have to be honest-our downtown is not very urban. I quickly realized it was a pretty pathetic setting for a legitimate hip-hop photo shoot. I was trying my best to make it appear super legit, so as to fit with the music, and it was just not happening. It looked like South Florida, but the nice retirement version. I was becoming more and more frustrated, because there was a certain visual image I wanted, and it definitely did not include silver-haired retirees walking in the background. So, we decided to switch locations.

I decided we need to move closer to the hood, near where I work. The plan was to hop out of the car real quick and take some killer pics with a legitimate background, but get in and out fast enough to avoid drawing too much attention. After thinking on it a bit, I decided on shooting near the train tracks. Keep in mind, I was pretty frustrated and somewhat desperate because we just didn't get what we needed downtown. So, we arrive at the tracks, and there was a train sitting there which must have been there a long time. It was bombed with graffiti art. And at that point I had started really delving into graffiti art, myself. In fact, my church had allowed me to do some pieces. They paid for my paint, and they would allow me to paint on the walls.

As I learned to paint, I submerged myself in graffiti culture. I learned the difference between tags, throw up's, pieces, and gang graffiti. So at the point of this story, I was entrenched enough in it that I understood all the different elements and styles. This is important to note, as you will see.

The paint on the train was called a "throw-up." This is a very simple piece, created quickly. It made perfect sense that it was a throw-up, and not a very intricate piece because we were very close to the main street. The train was in a very public area, so to simply walk up to it and shoot a few pictures was not a big deal. It wasn't private property, and it wasn't off the beaten path. It was perfectly legal for me to be there, so it seemed like an ideal setting.

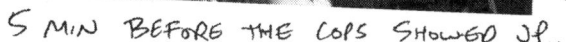
5 MIN BEFORE THE COPS SHOWED UP..

I liked the vibe. It captured the heart of the visuals I was going for. It looked much more urban than where I lived. I was excited, but as soon as we started capturing some good shots, I glanced back at the street and I saw lights blaring. It was a cop, of course. He gets out, gun on, his hand on his hip, undoing his holster.

At that time there was a style I was rocking that was common in hip-hop. The term we used was "backpack rapper," and the name was literal. The look and name came about from wearing a backpack. It was about function as much as form, as you wore the backpack everywhere; inside the bag was your rhyme book, some spray cans, etc. Only, I didn't have any spray paint on me at that moment.

So the cop says, freeze. My response was simply to ask what was going on. I literally worked down the street as a youth pastor, so I knew we weren't breaking any laws. I was clean as a whistle. But before I said anything, I tried to put down my backpack to reach in for my ID, per his request. He reacted immediately, and pulled his gun. I thought, I'm going to get shot standing here right now for no particular reason.

Then, things started getting out of hand, fast. Another cop pulled up, and then a third one, as well. They said, "We know what that is behind you."

I said, "It's a graffiti tag."

Then, they said, "No, it's gang graffiti."

And I looked at it, and I said, "That's a throw up. Like, that's not even close to gang graffiti." I wasn't trying to argue, but if you knew anything about graffiti, you would understand the difference. And it is a big difference.

The main cop said, "We're going to have to put you on the gang file for taking pictures with gang graffiti."

At that point I am thinking, this has to be a joke. I was a youth pastor with pastoral credentials, and I worked just down the street. They were trying to either shoot me, arrest me, or put me on the gang file. It was a high-crime neighborhood, do you know what I mean? Here I was doing absolutely nothing wrong, and there were probably ten other criminals violating the law within a few blocks of where we were. And here we were, me (the youth pastor), and my photographer (a well-dressed suburban kid).

They began running our IDs, and they made me pour out everything in my backpack. Mind you, this wasn't the first time something like this had happened to me. I had been pulled over previously for looking suspicious, and I had been stopped driving back from shows. I had my entire car torn apart and searched in the past. Because this had happened so many times I knew how to handle it. I had nothing to hide, so I told them they could search whatever they wanted. I wasn't belligerent, and I told them, all you are going to find are some Bibles and some Christian rap cds.

At first, the cops didn't buy it. So, I kept telling them I was a youth pastor. I said, I know my pants doesn't look like it, but look, that's what I do. But, more and more cops started showing up. About twenty minutes into it I was at a point where I was starting to get scared. I really thought I was going to get in trouble for literally doing nothing. So I started asking, did I trespass? Was I breaking the law? They just kept saying that I hadn't, but I was taking pictures with gang graffiti.

So, I said, again, "Sir, I'm not trying to convince you, but that's not gang graffiti. That's a tagging crew." But they wouldn't listen. So, my only option was to keep being nice and pray for a good outcome. I stuck to my guns, but I was also very compliant.

Finally, little by little, they started to realize we had nothing on us.

And as the tension started to ease, I started joking back and forth with the initial police officer. I asked him if I could go. But instead of just letting me go, he said he had to take our picture and put us in the gang file. He said they were required to by law. He told me he knew we weren't anything to be worried about, but they had to take a picture for their records. By that point I had actually signed a bunch of CDs and given them a bunch of free merchandise. So I made sure I said, hey guys, I just want to bless you with this.

Then I said, "Well, can we do a B-boy pose for my gang file picture?"

And they agreed.

And so we stood back to back with our arms crossed-like break dancers from the 1980's - and to this day that picture is probably still in the gang file.

CHAPTER 12
WEDDING DAY DISASTER

IN SPITE OF EVERYTHING GOING NUTS AT THE WEDDING, OUR RECEPTION WAS GREAT.

*"I couldn't even get into my wedding dress!
The lady sewed the sleeves together, and then the DJ couldn't even get our name right...
Mr. & Mrs. Sorrento... Sargento...Sorrentinio... NO! It's Mr & Mrs. Sorrentino."*
~ *Christa (kj's wife)*

Soundtrack for this chapter: "All My Life" KC and JoJo
(we danced our first dance to this song at our reception)

I knew within three weeks of dating my wife (then girlfriend) that I wanted to marry her. I wasn't just rushing in however, it's just that I knew, (but I also realized that the heart is deceitful above all things). I also knew that when you're in your twenties and you're Christian, you have a tendency to try to rush the wedding date because you're trying "remain pure". So we said we would wait six months to make sure our feelings were real. Six months came around and we decided to give it another six months. We said that if we still felt the same way after a year, then we would start talking about wedding plans. Then we waited another six months and we decided to fast and pray for another six months.

In the end, we went two years of dating before I finally decided that enough was enough! The problem was, I was still living at home. I wasn't even making enough money at my church job to even afford an apartment. Eventually I got a tiny raise, moved into a postage stamp-sized apartment, and started to get the ball rolling towards moving into the next phase of my life.

WE LOOK LIKE BABIES IN THIS PIC BUT I THINK IM 20 & SHES 18

One of the greatest things about my wife was that she had been with me through everything, including starting with a long distance relationship. When I was at Bible College, she stayed dating me until I moved back home after the first and only semester that I attended. She stayed with me when I volunteered at my local church as a youth pastor for two months. She was there with me through the years of working in the inner city of Ft. Myers, one of the toughest periods of my life. She was there with me for all of it.

So, we finally set a date, after we had been together for almost two and a half years at that point. We set the date for June, which in hindsight was a terrible idea because obviously that's one of the hottest times of the year in Florida. We settled on doing the ceremony at a church neither of us attended but loved the way it looked (more about why this was a bad idea later).

Flash forward to that day when of course, everything that could have gone wrong went wrong. I arrived at the church and I started putting on my Tuxedo. Then, I realized I never packed a bow tie! How could I look at the woman I love with no bow tie? Then, 16 year old Goldin Child, who was one of my groomsmen, showed up also with no bow tie, not thinking he even needed one. Then, my best man showed up with an actual bow tie… the only one in my wedding party who had one. I thought it couldn't get any worse.

Well, it did. It got worse.

It turned out the people responsible for my wife's wedding dress had sewn the arm shut so she couldn't even put it on. So there we were, several hours before the ceremony. I had no bow tie and she had no wedding dress. This was going to be a beautiful picture of our marriage for the next twenty-plus years. We would deal with adversity at every turn and try to figure out how to get through it.

The weird thing was, our relationship had started long distance, which, looking back, I realize was a picture of what it was going to be like as I traveled. God was preparing us, even though we didn't even realize it.

Somehow we got a couple of bow ties, and thanks to the Pastor's wife somehow she was able to get her wedding dress on. It was June, so we keep turning up the air conditioner in the church, and we could not figure out why it was so hot. It was stuffy and disgusting. It was Florida in June, but we were stuck inside with a couple hundred people in a small sanctuary.

Because of all the stuff that happened behind the scenes, the wedding started late. The moment when I saw her come down the aisle, I forgot about all of the issues.

THE CALM BEFORE THE STORM

There she was. We were looking at each other. We were exchanging our vows. And only a few minutes in, all of a sudden I heard a thud, and the entire crowd gasped. I looked around, super confused. I couldn't figure out what happened. And, I'll never forget the officiating pastor Dennis Gingerich looked over to me and said, "Your brother-in-law just passed out. That's okay. Keep going...He's fine."

Apparently, my younger brother-in-law (who was about nine years old), had locked his knees. It had been so hot in the room that he had fainted in the middle of the ceremony.

We didn't know it at the time, but the air conditioner was broken. The church had never bothered to actually tell us. And because it was so hot, when we went to light our unity candle (If you aren't aware of what this is, it involves three candles-one for the groom, one for the bride, and a third, which is lit by combining the other two flames), both of the candles had formed a pool of liquid wax. So when we turned to light the candle together, we actually put out the unity candle.

We had extinguished the flame of our marriage before it even began!

At that point, I thought, man, nothing else can go wrong. Then, I looked up and the officiating pastor left the stage. We were doing so bad, the pastor quit mid-ceremony, or at least that's what I thought. But actually, he left to get a candle lighter, and he lit the unity candle for us. Then, he leaned over and he whispered to both of us, "Just keep going."

So, we pushed through. And, you know, the reality of it was… despite all that had happened, it was a beautiful ceremony. Everyone loved it.

What Dennis, the pastor, said to us was the perfect picture of what marriage actually is; when everything goes wrong, sometimes all you can do is just keep going.

And we have kept going for over twenty years now.

STILL GOING STRONG ALL THESE YEARS LATER.

CHAPTER 13
HOW I WAS DISCOVERED

I THINK THIS WAS AT CREATION FEST... BUT HOW ON POINT IS MY EDGE UP HERE?

"When I first heard KJ's music, there was an intangible quality that I was drawn to that I couldn't quite explain. KJ turned out to be one of those rare artists that was very talented yet ultra driven to his calling. He always outworked his talent and I wanted to be connected to that." ~Todd Collins (Gotee records co-founder & producer)

Soundtrack to this chapter: "Integrity" kj52 ft. Teron from Grits

Around 1998, I started working on what would become my first solo record, Seventh Avenue. A sweet, little, old lady and her husband at my hood church gave me $2,000 to record and press the album, which I planned to give away in my youth ministry and in the streets. At least that was the plan. The problem was, I spent all the money on the recording itself. In other words, I went way over budget. All the while, I was still working at the church as an inner city youth pastor, barely scraping up enough money to pay rent and food. Little by little, though, I was feeling restless. I was ready for the next chapter to start.

I felt like hip-hop was what I was supposed to be doing full-time, but it was not something that could just happen over night. It just doesn't work that way. There was no training program for me to go off to with a potential job placement of "full time rapper" coming afterward. God had to do something to make it a reality. And at that time, in 1998, all I wanted to do was go out and share my faith through my music, I just didn't know how it was going to happen. I ran out of money making my first record, while working at the church making about $7.50 an hour. I didn't even have the money to press the tapes and give them away–which was the reason I was given the money in the first place.

I remember sitting in my apartment, frustrated, not knowing what to do racking my brain trying to figure out what the next step should be. Then, I felt that still small voice telling me to be obedient and step out in faith, trusting that God would provide. I shared this with my wife, and it subsequently turned into a pretty intense argument about finances and the future. Her point was that we didn't have the money to afford it. She kept asking how I was going to pay for my music career. I just sat there, dejected. I felt like a failure. I felt like I let my wife down, as well as the people who invested in me, and I had not accomplished what I was supposed to do.

She walked out. It was a tense moment that I'll never forget it. A few moments later, she walked right back in. She looked me in the eye and she said, "If God told you to do it, then do it."

And that was all I needed to hear.

So, I put the money on a credit card, and threw caution to the wind. Around this time I was thinking I should probably get a record deal. That would have enabled me to press the tapes and give them away. And it was almost like God was telling me to trust him, then he would give me everything I was looking for, and so much more.

I started sending out demos of the album to multiple record labels, including Gotee records. They were in the mix for me because I had done a song with Teron from Grits. When we cut that track, I got in contact with Gotee to get approval on the song. Truth be told, I was hoping some one would hear it and give me a record deal.

I kept sending off demo tape after demo tape to many different record labels, to the tune of zero response back. Nobody paid me any attention, no one was going to give me a deal. Again, I knew I was going to have to trust God. So I said I would press the record myself and trust that God would meet me halfway as I did this huge endeavor.

I'll never forget sitting at the dinner table with my wife when my cell phone rang. I rarely used my phone because it was so expensive. So, when it rang, I paused. I remember, clear as day, because I was eating chicken. It was kind of greasy. I answered the phone. And on the other end was Todd Collins from Gotee records. He said, "I just found your demo, and I'd really like to get to know more about you."

Todd co-owned the label with Joey Elwood and Toby Mac.
I couldn't believe it. I came to find out years later he had actually been walking by an intern's office, who was playing my demo tape. He didn't actually go into the office at the time. Instead, he came back and took my demo to his car and listened to it. He liked it, and he called me on the spot.

Now, I have to tell you that nobody gets signed off of sending in a demo like that. It is so incredibly rare. For him to call me, and for this to actually happen in this sort of manner, there is no way to attribute it to anything but divine appointment. The situation checked all the boxes of what I was looking for. He flew down and met me, came to a couple of shows and saw what I was doing in the inner city with the project kids.

I took him on a tour through the hood and showed him what I was about. We kept in touch, but one month turned into two months, and two months turned to three. Three months turned into four months. The time dragged out, and I was becoming more and more frustrated. I thought I was going to get strung along and the deal would never come through. I waited nearly six months.

If you can imagine being that close to your dream, and yet still being so far, you can imagine how I felt. I was in agony. At one point, I remember Todd called me and said, point blank, "Look, Gotee is not going to sign you. They're going to go with John Reuben over you." Then, he said, "But I have a whole other record label that I've been talking to, and they want to get into the Christian hip-hop industry. They are a mainstream CCM label, and they're called Essential records." Essential had Jars of Clay, Third Day and artists like that. He said, "They want you to be their first signing, and they're going to come down and check you out."

I was skeptical at first, but things moved fairly quickly. Within a couple months I had signed the deal. A couple more months after that I was in Nashville, living in a hotel for about a month straight, getting all the ducks in a row for my album to finally come out, which it did a couple months later.

And then, within a couple months more, I got dropped from the label for low record sales. Did you catch all that? In nine months total I went from unsigned to signed to debuting my album to being dropped. My head was spinning. I mean, my shelf life was so short. The album came out in June, and I was dropped by September. So much of my experience in this industry has been about getting really close and then fumbling, then getting really close, and then just fumbling, and then getting really close again.

PROVIDENT MUSIC GROUP

June 27, 2001

VIA CERTIFIED MAIL
RETURN RECEIPT REQUESTED

Jonah Sorrentino
1031 SE 9th Street #16
Cape Coral, Florida 33990

Re: Option on Exclusive Recording Agreement

Dear Jonah,

This letter serves as written notification by Brentwood Music, Inc. d/b/a Essential Records to you that Essential Records hereby elects not to exercise the first option as provided in paragraph 5B of the Exclusive Recording Agreement dated August 9, 1999 and entered into by and between you and Brentwood Music, Inc. d/b/a Essential Records.

We thank you for your dedication to your music and ministry. May God continue to bless you in all that lies ahead.

Best regards.

Sincerely,

THE ACTUAL LETTER, AND NO I DON'T LIVE THERE ANYMORE SO DON'T VISIT ME!

I spent about a year just struggling to get by, and no record labels would touch me. They viewed me as a broken experiment.

Then, out of nowhere, Tooth and Nail called me. They were a rock label, and Brandon Ebel offered me a record deal that I couldn't turn down. He offered me what was called a non-exclusive deal, meaning I could sign with them, and still sign with somebody else at the same time, if I chose to. And I thought to myself, well, this will just be something good that I'll do for now until I can get a bigger record deal.

My second album, which was Collaborations, was my first release on Tooth and Nail. That was the record "Dear Slim" was on.

I had gone to every single Nashville CCM label with a carefully thought out plan for my second album. My plan was to switch up my image. My plan was to record "Dear Slim," and I had a very clear idea of what I was going to do. Yet, none of the CCM labels would touch me. It took a rock label out of Seattle that was known for putting out hardcore punk music that decided to gamble on me.

And that gamble paid off with massive dividends. Then, three years later, my first label, Essential, tried to resign me.

I promptly said, "No."

CHAPTER 14
SPELLS, WARLOCKS, AND SKATE KIDS

2ND SHOW OF THE FIRST TOUR, I THINK THERE WAS MAYBE 10 PEOPLE THERE.

"*Arggggghhhhhhhhhhh!!!!!*" Skate kid in Lincoln City OR
(right before he tried to hit me with his board)

Soundtrack to this chapter: 1, 2, 3 by Kj52 (7th avenue)

Right around 2000, when my first album came out, there wasn't a ton of opportunities for me to go full time with my music. It all didn't happen overnight. But, the one opportunity that did come my way was an outreach tour in the Northwest called the Xtreme Tour. And when I say Northwest, I mean Idaho, Oregon, and Washington-which was a loooong way from Florida. I should mention the fact that I was not getting paid. In other words, I was playing strictly for merchandise sales. Going into it, I was thinking…how am I even going to afford to make it out there?

So, I booked a handful of shows that would get me all the way to the Northwest. But, every drive was about twelve hours between shows, which is brutal, in hindsight. I really didn't care at the time because I was just living my dream for the first time. I had a record in stores, and I was all-in on going for it.

I quit my job at the Census Bureau, loaded my wife and my DJ in my minivan, and said we're going to do this. We worked our way out west on minimal paid shows. We arrived at the first date-and you have to keep in mind-I hadn't done a ton of outreach shows. I also had never experienced the northwest. I had no idea what the vibe was going to be like, and I didn't know what the philosophy of the culture was. I had lived one entire summer in Idaho, but that was about it.

MY WIFE HOLDING DOWN THE MERCH TABLE

This was just like nothing I had ever experienced.

I arrive, and the lineup consisted of all rock bands. I was the only rapper on the tour. I had just left youth ministry, and everyone on the tour elected me to do the altar call each night, since they perceived me as the most spiritually mature of the whole crew.

The whole idea behind the tour was kind of unorthodox. The tour basically would set up a stage at a skate park or a place where kids were already hanging out, then we just started playing live music all day. The show culminated with me finishing out the night and sharing the gospel. On paper it sounded fine. But when it came down to the execution, it was an absolute nightmare. We would show up at "venues" and there would be ten kids at a skate park, and they wouldn't really be down for our presence there. They would get mad and say, why are you making noise in our skate park?

It was a very sink or swim moment every day, because it was basically a mission trip and there weren't built-in merchandise sales guaranteed.

The weird thing was, in Idaho, the shows were filled with Mormon kids, and they were actually super excited for us to be there. So, we saw all these LDS kids come out and participate in the event, and some even gave their lives to Christ. In other words, one of the Idaho shows actually went well. Let me make it clear, though: there was absolutely nothing glamorous about this tour. My DJ, my wife, and I were the only ones on the tour that were actually able to stay in a host home. Everyone else on the tour slept on floors at a local church. And, it's not like I had earned the host home, either. The tour was just taking pity on us because my wife and I were newlyweds.

As you can imagine, sleeping in someone's house you have never met before with your brand new wife was an…adventure. I won't go into too much detail on that, but let's just say it was very much a time of "stretching."

As we began to move into Oregon, again, I had no cultural context. All I knew at that point in my life was Florida. I didn't know how unchurched Oregon was. I didn't know anything about those areas of the country. All I knew was that I was trying to reach kids, and I had to do whatever it took to accomplish that.

I'll never forget, you know, we set up at the Skate Park in Lincoln City, Oregon. As the rock bands were playing, there were no problems. But the minute I went onstage and opened my mouth to talk about Jesus, I remember one of the skaters screaming as loud as he could, literally trying to drown me out. I had never experienced that much opposition to the Gospel before, at least not in that type of setting. And the longer I went, the more agitated they became. This culminated with him coming at me with his skateboard. He was actually going to bash me over the head with it! Two of the kids that had gotten saved the night before turned around and were ready to fight him.

THIS WAS MINUTES BEFORE I WAS ATTACKED.

So, picture this: I'm at a skate park. I'm rapping, I'm sharing Jesus. One guy is trying to hit me while another is trying to hit him, while a third is screaming at the top of his lungs. That was like day fourteen on the tour. I asked myself, what have I gotten myself into with this tour? And then I get to sleep at a stranger's house and I probably made fifty dollars in merchandise. I'm slowly going into debt. I left everything to do this, and my record isn't selling. And the pressure of all this is coming down on me more and more the further we get into the tour. I didn't see any way it would end on a good note, from a financial or career standpoint.

When all of this hit me, I was forced to change my philosophy. So, when we would roll up to the next skate park, I would immediately go around and make friends with all the kids. I would give my music out. I would try to be their homie. I promised to give them some free stuff. So, by the time I actually got on the stage, I had already kind of won over the crowd. It really shifted the tide of how I was able to connect with the audience.

If you have ever seen my live show, it's very interactive. That was born out of necessity because of situations like that one.

I couldn't just get up there and do ten songs for a crowd of people who didn't know my music. I started incorporating my freestyle, as well as call and response stuff. I remixed my beats with secular, well-known instrumentals. I tailored my whole show around connecting with new audiences, grabbing their attention, and keeping their attention so I could minister the Gospel to them.

One night we set up for a show in Seattle. I looked out, and the place was just filled with homeless kids. Out of the corner of my eye, I saw this guy in a cape. No joke. And every time I spoke or performed, he spread open his cape. It was some kind of weird Batman gesture. All in all things were chill. I went through the crowd and played hacky-sack with the homeless kids. No one was trying to kill me with a skateboard like the show in Oregon. But as I got offstage, I asked people what was up with the dude with the cape. And one kid said, "Oh, he's been casting spells on you the entire time you've been performing. And, apparently, it's not working."

I thought to myself, I've hit a whole new level in my career. I've had my life threatened. I was nearly attacked with a skateboard. And now, a warlock is trying to get me.

All of it started to take a toll on me, physically. We wrapped up the tour in Spokane, Washington. By then, I was just physically sick with the flu. We pulled up into the parking lot of a Catholic bookstore, and there were literally five people there. I was sick. I was broke. I had no shows on the horizon. And I was thinking, I'm about to get dropped by the label. This can't get any worse.

I remember saying that I was too sick to do the altar call that night, that I was just going to play my music and then die (not literally but I felt like it). I had become super negative by the final show. I thought, the same five Christian kids will get saved tonight, like they always do. I was just in such a terrible place. I took a walk then came back, and it felt like God was impressing on me

Do what you are called to do…

I think the crowd swelled to maybe eight people. I did my thing and I gave my little message. Two kids came forward. I was super negative, still, inside of it. I thought, yeah, they probably get saved every time there's an event here. I felt like the tour was the worst decision I ever made. Then, I went to sit behind my merch table, utterly dejected. I sat down and I thought, why am I even doing this? No one is going to buy anything.

Then one of the guys from the tour brought the two kids over to me. He said, "Hey! You don't know this, but they were walking by and heard the music and they were going to go get drugs and get high. And they heard it and they stopped. And this guy gave his life to Christ for the first time."

I just sat there, stunned. I had been such a terrible vessel for God to work through. In spite of that, he still did something. I started talking to one of the guys and gave him my contact information. Flash forward a year later, and I was still in touch with him. Then, I found out his father passed away a little while later. But, a church just began to really love on him and his friend. And we stayed in touch for years and years.

That kid, the same kid who that night went to go get drugs, eventually ended up becoming a missionary in Germany. I look back on that moment and realize that all of those trials were for a reason. They taught me how to become a better performer, a better minister, and a better artist. But really, what that experience taught me was to be ready in season and out of season. I learned that I have to be faithful, even in the little things. While those first two years of my career were the hardest I ever dealt with, I look back and I wouldn't change a single thing, because it taught me so much.

CHAPTER 15
DEAR SLIM

I had to write this backward to get this effect...

"I appreciate the prayers but I already got God on my side.." Eminem

Soundtrack to this chapter: Dear Slim pt. 2

When I was jumping into the battle circuit, Goldinchild and I were heading to South Beach. We went to Dj Khaled's pirate radio station where we were supposed to open up for a mainstream rap group called The Beatnuts. One of the guys who was part of the crew was named A.L. He said to me, "Yo, man. You gotta check out my boy Eminem from Detroit."

We were freestyling live on the air for a mainstream station. I was in the moment. And I just remember thinking in the back of my head, Yeah, dude, another white rapper... who cares?

He quoted me one of his lyrics, and I was really not very impressed. I remember thinking very clearly...no white rapper from Detroit is ever going to make it. At that time, hip-hop was ultra regional

Flash forward a year or so, and I was starting to put my stuff in stores on consignment, really hustling. I was all in on the independent tip. I remember going into a store and seeing his tape right there on the counter, and it was free. So, I ended up taking one. I remember listening to it on the way back home and thinking, this is just pure white-boy shock rap. I mean, you could not deny the skills, but in my head I was just thinking about all the challenges that I faced for being a white rapper. I questioned if he would ever be accepted.

White rappers in the nineties kind of had to fall into one of a few very neat categories. You were either a rap/rock guys (like the Beastie boys), or you were a crazy ethnic rapper (like House of Pain), or you were the underground white boys like 3rd Bass. So, I pondered shock rap from a white guy's perspective. In my mind, the rapper would have to be so out there that people just wouldn't think to test him. So, I sat back and observed Eminem's career, watching to see if it would actually work.

I recorded my album in 1998, and his album came out in 1999. I had been sitting on my indie album, which eventually became Seventh Avenue two years later on a major label. So it was 2000 by the time it dropped, and Eminem had already been out for a bit.

I remember performing at this spot in Texas. This was the first time I ever heard anybody say that I sounded like Eminem. People were talking about me, and I just shrugged it off, chalking it up to typical white rapper comparisons that I had dealt with for years. But, little by little this began to happen over and over and over. And I thought, if you're telling me that I'm just trying to copy Eminem that's impossible. My record was started a year before his ever came out. There was no way I had a plan to copy him. And I never had the intention to be the Christian version of him, even after the fact, even if the Christian market has a habit of branding artists as the faith-based version of another artist.

I really took my craft very seriously, especially from an MC perspective. So the more this began to happen, the more I began to get frustrated. I said, the only way for me to really handle this is just to address it in a song. It was very popular back then to do the mix tape thing, where you take the other person's beat and then you rap over their beat to address them. I said, I'm not going to go and dis Eminem. I am going to just address this whole thing in a song. We were from similar backgrounds, only I had found Christ. I went over it many times in my head and I felt like this was the best way to kill the noise, so to speak.

So, that truly is all "Dear Slim" was. I wrote it in 2000, never intending to put it out.

Flash-forward a couple of months and I got dropped from my label. I was floating around label-less for a year, trying to get back into the industry. I ended up performing "Dear Slim" one, single time, and people lost their minds the first time I performed it. I was blown away because the song didn't even have a hook. The verses were super long, and I was convinced it would never work at radio. Yet, somehow or another the song struck a nerve that I had never experienced before. People kept coming up to me asking me, where can I hear that song, when are you going to put it out? So, when I finally got my second record deal with Tooth and Nail, I had to release the song just because of the demand for it.

Again, there was never any real intention behind the track, truth be told. I didn't even think he would ever even hear it. I finally got around to recording it and I put it out in 2001. I was just struggling to pay bills. I was rocking as many shows as I could. A couple of weeks after it came out, a guy walked up to me and he said, "Hey, you don't know me, but last night I was at the Video Music Awards and I gave Eminem your album."

He went on to tell me how he was there as a road pastor for POD. He had prayed, and he saw all Eminem's bodyguards just disappear right afterwards. Like, they walked away.

He walked up to him and said, "Hey, you know that Song 'Stan?'"

Eminem responded, "Yeah."

He said, "Well, this guy right here, he's got a song like that. It's similar, but he has a message for you."

And Eminem asked, "Well, is he dissing me in the song?"

The road pastor said, "No, he's just got something you need to hear in it."

So he took the CD and he walked out with it.

My mind was blown because there was no way I ever thought in a million years he would ever hear it. It was direct evidence that God can do some amazing things with unamazing people, and carry things to places you might never imagine.

Flash-forward a couple more months, we shot the video, we dropped the video, we sent the video off to MTV2 (not thinking they'll ever play it), and then we forgot all about it. I was in traffic in Toronto, Canada, when I get a phone call from the record label. They told me that MTV's TRL was going to play my video that very day and they were going to make it controversial.

I was on the phone with my wife, and she was holding it up to the TV set so I could hear what's happening. So, I sat there and listened to the hosts of TRL rip me apart. They talked about how I dissed Eminem. I couldn't believe it.

And I thought, well, this is where it's all going to end. This song will never go any further than this point.

Jump ahead just a couple of years and I am getting dissed by Christian and mainstream rappers over the whole thing. So, I wrote the "Dear Slim, Part Two," to sum up what I wanted to say a little bit better and put the whole thing to bed. It was never about a gimmick, or trying to make lightning strike twice, just to be perfectly clear, again.

Then, I received an email from a prison guard which said, "Hey, you don't know me, but I've been sharing the gospel with Kim Mathers, Eminem's ex-wife, in jail, and I would like to give her your music."

So, I said I would go one step further. And, I began to write her letters while she was in jail. The best thing about it was, the guy gave it to her in the jail cell. He would print them off and hand it to her, then tell me what she said back. I was having this conversation with Kim Mathers through this prison guard, and he played my songs, and even played "Dear Slim" for her. He told me one of the songs actually brought her to tears, and how much she appreciated the line that I was praying for her and Eminem.

I promised myself I was not going to use this story to give myself a pat on the back. So, I kept it quiet for years. I never told anybody about it. And all the while I was getting dragged through the mud in the headlines. Then, VH1 decided to put out a show called The 40 Least Moments in Hip-hop, and they make me number twenty-six, simply for praying for Eminem and trying to be a light in all this.

Wow.

I have had this turmoil over the whole thing because, again, it was something I just wrote on a whim, not thinking it would ever get to him. But, he and Kim Mathers, they are real people that need Jesus just like I do. The minute I start to become a person who tries to exploit someone's celebrity for my own gain, I've missed the point.

Again, I thought the whole thing was over at that point.

You flash forward a couple more years, I get another email and it says, "Hey, you don't know this, but guess what? I think Eminem just responded to your 'Dear Slim' song."

Keep in mind, this is nine years after I wrote it, and he talked about it in a song titled "Be Careful What You Wish For."

In the song he tells the story of a fan who had been praying for him, and how that had been weighing on his mind heavy. And you know, he said he appreciated the prayers, but he already had God on his side.

I can't say for certain that line is about me, but it sure sounds like it. Again, it was never about anything except for just trying to share who Christ was in my life. But, maybe in a small way it felt like a validation. The irony about the whole situation from top to bottom is that it really just shows that God can do anything with the most insignificant people. Also, He has the ability to take the insignificant things we do, little lyrics we scribble on a piece of paper and blow it up bigger than we could ever imagine. If you would have told me a song that I wrote at 2:00 AM in 2000 would put me on the biggest platform possible and that it would connect me with the biggest rapper of all time, I would have said you are crazy.

But that's exactly what God does.
He does some amazing things with very unamazing people.

CHAPTER 16
SCRIBBLE JAM

SOMEONE SHOULD HAVE DISSED ME FOR WEARING A SKINNY w/ A POLO .. FASHION NONO.

"You aint hard... you more like hardly..
you hardly even rapping and you're hardly an emcee.."
~ Kj52 (Spit and Spin Battle Contest)

Soundtrack to this chapter: "Say what ya want" kj52 (yearbook album)

I think one thing that definitely drew me to hip hop from the jump was the competitiveness of it. My fire to compete inside of the culture truly began with break dancing in the early 80's. As a Catholic school kid, I can definitely remember myself and all my peers trying to outdo one another by doing whatever terrible break dance move we could think of. Little did I know that the foundation was being laid for me during those ridiculous dance sessions.

I was drawn to the competitiveness before I even dabbled in battle rap. When I first started writing with my first "rhyme partner," Greg aka Pigs from The G-Force Posse, I used to call him constantly to try to battle him on the telephone. I think there was a competitive spirit in me to begin with; I always tried to do whatever I did at the highest level. Not that I was ever particularly great at any particular thing, but I was just born with the idea of wanting to be number one. So, I think the battle aspect of hip-hop appealed to me because it's my nature to want to go for the top spot.

I started becoming fascinated with freestyling in the late 80's. This was during the time many refer to as the golden era of hip hop. Back then, freestyling was a rite of passage for an emcee in many ways. I look back and realize that some of those guys were just spitting verses that they had already memorized but no one had ever heard of. At the time, I thought they were making it up on the spot. So I got sucked into this idea that in order to be a rapper you were supposed to be able to freestyle. Even at a very young age my dad put me in Improv classes and I learned to perform skits and do impromptu theater. So, while I wasn't some child prodigy freestyle kid, I definitely vibed with the idea of being spontaneous in the realm of performance.

A couple of years later, I came to Christ, and my whole perspective changed. So I tried to reconcile what it meant to be in a genre that is super competitive and self-centered with the Jesus worldview that says it's not about you.

Right before I came to Christ, I remember I was working in the back room at my first job in North Michigan. I thought, I wonder if I could freestyle? For some reason I also thought, I wonder what it would be like if I tried to do it about God. I had struggled with freestyling up to that point. But for some reason, once I started-and you have to know I had a very limited knowledge of who God was at the time-these gorgeous lines began to flow. Afterward, I filed the experience away in the bank of my mind and thought, well that was weird…

Jump ahead a couple of years, and I started to travel to do shows. I began to live the dream, even if it was just a guy in a Honda Civic driving all over Florida, slinging tapes out of my trunk. I was really starting to become part of the hip-hop culture. As things began to progress, eventually it led to starting a group with Goldin Child.

I remember we played a show at a church where a pastor said, you need to go cast your net on the other side of the boat. I interpreted this as I needed to get into some of the more secular arenas. At that point, I had messed around with various open mics, but I never made a concentrated effort to be in the clubs, participating in the battle contests. Honestly I was struggling with how to do battle rap while still maintaining my faith. I had a hard time seeing if it was even possible.

By 2002, at that time, I had just signed my second record deal. So, I was touring and things were finally starting to turn around. I was very concerned that I was going to be stuck in the Christian rap bubble and I would never be able to continue to sharpen my skills. Previously, Goldin Child and I would sort of "fake" battle one another all the time to keep each other sharp. Freestyle, at that point, was very much part of our show. Fast forward a couple more years, and Eight Mile came out. All of a sudden, battle rapping became the cool thing to do. It became very popular, but it was actual, freestyle battle rapping. It was spontaneous. Today it is pre-written and rehearsed. Back then, it was the era where you squared off, and you didn't know anything about who you were going up against. You didn't even know what beats you would have to rhyme on. You had about thirty seconds, and it was definitely all in the moment. And, if you came with something pre-written to a battle, you would get eaten up.

So, there was this local battle contest. I really struggled with how to approach it because, on one hand, I needed to be a light in the darkness. I wondered how I could actually do that, though, when on the other hand the whole point was to win.

So, I actually went and met with my pastor and I said, hey, you know, I'm, I'm trying to figure out how to make this happen. God bless my pastor, because he said you just need to "snap" on him. At the time I was attending a church in the middle of the hood. It was just part of our culture to make fun of each other, but in a way that was creative. He told me to take the approach of avoiding curses, but otherwise still giving the other guy a good, clever roast. I don't know too many pastors who understood hip-hop culture enough to give you the green light to battle, along with a game plan, but that's exactly what he did.

So, I had a bunch of rebuttals memorized, meaning I knew they were going to come at me for being white. I also knew they were going to compare me to Eminem. So, I was ready. What I had learned up to that point was that the key to being a great battle rapper was to be able to exist in the moment, but also have a few rounds in the chamber. Let it be known, all of my punch lines were meant to be clever without being hateful or ungodly.

So I enter the battle, and lo and behold, I blew through all the competition, all the way down to the very end. Throughout the whole thing I got booed, new lines were thrown at me, but eventually, I pulled in the crowd. They couldn't deny all my years of practicing freestyle. It just came right out of me.

I got the footage of the battle, and sent it off to one of most preeminent freestyle battle competitions at the time. It was called Scribble Jam. A couple of years prior, Eminem battled in it, and eventually got his record deal as a result. So, it was a very prestigious hip-hop event. And as far as I knew up to that point, not a single Christian hip-hop artist had ever even remotely tried to enter. So, I sent them my footage, thinking I will just give it a try. To my surprise, I was picked! Myself and fifteen others were chosen to go to Cincinnati for the event. So, I ended up scraping the money together and flew up there.

And at that point, I changed my mode of attack. My plan was not to rip rappers apart, win their respect, and then tell them about Jesus. No, I knew I was going to be up front in my approach, but I was also not going to be whack. Does that make sense? I was approaching it as legitimately as possible without compromising my identity as a Christian.

What actually ended up happening is I lost in the first round.

Then, I took it upon myself to go online on my own website and vent a little bit. To be honest, I felt like I had been given a raw deal. The next thing I knew, some of the secular hip-hop outlets picked up my blog. And I got ripped up and down. They basically said I was a Christian coming in with all these presumptions without respecting the culture. Remember, there was already a huge backlash from the Christian rap world toward me. And various pockets of that side of the industry were lighting me up, as well. The basic sentiment was…of all the people to represent our world, "KJ52-Youth Group, Eminem wannabe rapper" is not the one…

I learned a lot from the fallout. First, I learned the world was listening to me vent on my website. Second, you have to check your motives when you react and post online. And, three, sometimes you just got to take the "L" and keep it moving. You have to learn from your mistakes….and not vent about losing on your own website.

So, I applied everything from my mistakes. Then, a new local battle contest started in my town every Tuesday night. Goldin Child and I started going there all the time. The irony was, we kept winning. I mean, I would win the freestyle contest one night, and he might win the battle contest, or vice versa. It got to the point that we were winning so much that they offered me a job at the local secular radio station. We built a reputation as these two Christian kids who will rip you, then give you a hug, and never cuss once.

The thing was, a lot of the battles didn't always end well. Sometimes the crowd would get mad. But, I ended up being able to speak to the guys I battled offstage and build relationships with them. I was able to not only let my light shine on stage, but offstage as well. I realized in a lot of ways battling is like being a boxer. If I walk up to you on the street and I punch you in the face, I'm going to go to jail. But, if we decide with certain rules and parameters to square off against each other, then it's more of a sport than it is anything else. Two Christians can battle each other in this context, or a nonbeliever could also box a believer. And that's really how I view battling-I conduct myself as a believer in that context, but I certainly go in there to win. At first glance, it sounds like a contradiction. But it actually is not, because we are dealing with two distinctly separate ideas. I can have a problem with division and gossip and mean-spirited talk from Christians to each other. I also can take issue if other people say something publicly about me without saying it to my face. I have a huge problem with those things. But, I don't have a problem with Christians battling because it's face to face, man to man, with the agreed upon rules of sport.

I'm actually so excited for this next generation of battle rappers, because these guys are going in a completely different direction. They are delving into apologetics. They are literally defending the faith as they step in the arena. The battle world is a very lonely, empty place, and in many ways you function like a navy seal. You go behind enemy lines, and you have to survive. A navy seal can prepare the way for the army to win. And I believe battle rap, when it's approached the right way by a believer, can truly prepare the way for people to know Christ.

CHAPTER 17
DOVE AWARDS

I took this pic right after I won, it sort of puts things in perspective..

"I want to thank the pioneers of gospel hip hop who never got acknowledged for paving the way.. I would not be here today if it wasn't for them.."
~ kj52 (dove award acceptance speech 2007)

Soundtrack for this chapter: It's pronounced five two kj52 lp (my first award)

I remember very clearly going to the Dove Awards in 1996. If you don't know what I am referring to, the Dove's are the Christian music equivalent of the Grammy's. So for me, coming up, it was a dream of anyone in my position for someone to recognize your music enough to win one.

I had just finished a semester of Bible college and someone had given me a press pass to attend the Dove Awards in Nashville TN. I was only twenty-two, not a member of the press, and my Dove Award badge had a girl's name on it. So, I crashed the event mainly because I was starving, there was free food, and I wanted to get backstage and pass off my demo to get a record deal.

The biggest problem I saw in the industry back then was that Christian hip-hop was almost an afterthought. They would combine the hip-hop category with other Dove categories such as dance music and nominate CCM artists who weren't even rappers, but might have had an 8 bar rap on a song they did. Inevitably, for years, rappers didn't even get nominations in this "category."

In other words, actual rappers never won Dove Awards in the category for rap.
So, there was a constant frustration in the sense that Christian music was never going to acknowledge what Christian hip-hop truly was; we were treated like the redheaded stepchild of the industry.

Flash-forward a couple of years to when I got my first record deal. I had gotten dropped right away, floated for a year to get a new record deal, and then experienced gigantic turn around success. At the time I didn't think I would ever get a Dove Award because I felt like the same stigma was always going to be attached to Christian hip-hop. But then, Grits started to win, and I started to feel as if there was hope, because I viewed Grits as a legitimate pioneering Christian hip hop group.

It wasn't until 2002-when they finally gave Christian hip hop it's own category- that I won my first award. I'll never forget that moment, because it had little to do with winning the actual Dove Award. It had more to do with the fact that my wife was with me in the crowd. I say that because of the amount of sacrifice we had to go through to get to that point.

HEISMAN POSE!

I felt like I put her through pure hell on so many levels.

So, to know that my wife was with me, cheering me on, in 2002, when I was able to walk onto that stage was just incredible. I won for It's Pronounced Five-Two, which was my third album. Just to know she saw it, made it all worth it. I mean, we had been evicted from our apartment, we had our car repossessed, we had gone into severe financial debt and we were just starting to see the light at the end of the tunnel.

I mean it was just problem after problem, and to finally turn the corner, to finally be acknowledged by your peers, was phenomenal.

The only problem was I started to get backlash over this, of course. An undercurrent began to grow which said, KJ is only winning Dove Awards because he's white. I started to read articles about myself which labeled the CCM industry as racist because, again, I was a white guy winning the Christian Rap Dove Award category. There were plenty of other black guys and Hispanics that won the category way before me, but it didn't really matter. It was about perception, and perception is reality.

Then I just started winning one after another, almost every year.

I WAS A LITTLE BIT HAPPY.

It reached a point where I felt I wasn't really deserving of an award. At one point I won a Dove Award for the best album (which was a remix album) and I felt as if it was not fair. Especially because Lecrae was in the mix, and he was really starting to bubble up. I felt like he didn't get the Dove because he didn't have the record label machine behind him to help out with the voting process. But, if you compared both of our records from a sales standpoint, he deserved to win. I will never forget this because after that I made it a point on the following acceptance speech to thank all the Christian hip-hop pioneers... and, that's exactly what I did.

I read off a list of all the guys that had come before me, all the Christian hip-hop pioneers who would never be acknowledged in the same way that I got acknowledged. The irony of the whole moment was that when I won that fourth or fifth Dove, there was a mix-up backstage. When I went to receive my award, they didn't have it ready. So, they gave me a blank one and told me to hold onto it until they could get me the real one. Eventually they gave me the actual award, then they told me I could hang onto the blank one as well. And I was thinking, what am I going to do with an extra blank Dove Award?

I went home, and a couple months passed. Out of nowhere I got another blank Dove Award in the mail. It made no sense. So, I had four or five real ones, and two extra blank ones. And I remember when I won, I remember kind of walking by Lecrae and I just saw the frustration on his face. I saw all the frustration that I had felt for the ten years prior in one man's face.

I told myself I was going to right the wrongs that were never righted for the industry for those previous years.

So, I ended up getting his address but didn't tell him what I was going to do. I took my two blank ones, I went to a trophy shop and I put his name on both of them. I gave him the categories of best song and best album, and I mailed them to him. And I just put a little note in there that said, hey, if you never get a dove, I just want you to know that I acknowledge everything about what your ministry and your music is about.

I felt at that point in the Christian hip-hop industry, we had gotten too competitive. I felt we weren't cheering each other on, we weren't taking the time to lift each other up. It's very easy in hip-hop to be all about the competition. And I thought, the Kingdom of God is bigger than that.

He called me right after he got the awards, and he was just blown away. He couldn't believe I did it. And I just said, "listen, no one needs to know about this. I didn't do this for anyone else except for you. Just to tell you that if you never get one, you got two of mine."

I prayed for him, and it was interesting because it shifted our connection. Up to that point we never worked on music together, there wasn't really enough of a connection to pull that off. Something about that moment changed things. Within a year or two we ended up doing our first track together, which was called, "They like me." Against all odds, Christian hip-hop has prevailed in an industry that used to keep it completely pushed to the side.

It's weird to see how well embraced it is now. In fact, in a lot of ways it kicked Christian rock music out of the Pantheon.

And I'll never get another Dove award again. I'm sure I won't.

I never actually displayed any of mine at home to be honest. My wife put them up above my mantle at one point. I have one that's sitting in the garage. The last one I got when I went to give my acceptance speech, I held it up and the bottom fell out of it. It literally fell out. It was such a weird indication of where the music industry was. I said in my backstage press run, literally, the bottom has fallen out of my Dove Award and the bottom has fallen out of the music industry.

It was just strangely symbolic of where the music industry has gone. And it's weird to say that now, as an independent artist, I have more freedom. I have more hookups and more connections than I ever have.

To be acknowledged by your peers is great, but to be acknowledged for building God's kingdom trumps any Dove Award I may ever have.

CHAPTER 18
CHRISTIAN RAP BEEF

"Being the number one Christian Rapper is like saying you're the tallest short man.." kj52

Soundtrack to this chapter: Say what ya want kj52 (yearbook)

Right around the time I released the song "Dear Slim" I started noticing a backlash against me in the Christian hip-hop community. This was back in 2004/2005, when the internet had just started gaining steam with social media. Christian rap forums, labels, and websites were all in their infant stages. So, it became possible for the industry to congregate as a community in a brand new way. For the first time, people could post opinions without actually being there with them in person. Everyone discovered that the anonymity of the Internet allowed anyone to say what was actually on their mind without the threat of having to deal with direct confrontation or physical, human interaction.

I started building relationships with other Christian rappers as early as the mid-nineties. There was an event that was called Cruvention back in the day, which was the first Christian rapper convention. The lesson learned from that event was, the more Christian rappers you get together, the more problems occurred. Don't get me wrong- no fights ever broke out. But, people would group up based on their methodology and arguments ensued, beefs started, and battles would erupt.

You have to understand, I was never the guy to run into a crowded room and yell fire. That is just not my personality. I wasn't even the guy to even pick sides, usually. This goes way back to the way I was in high school, where I really was friends with everybody, every group, every clique. I hung out with the jocks. I was cool with the theater kids. I got along with the band kids. As a Christian rapper in the mid to late nineties, I was the same way.

If I am honest, there has been division for the last twenty years in the Christian rap community, probably before I even got into the game. So again, I was always the guy who tried to be cool with everybody, from the super theology rappers to the battle rappers to the average dude trying to fit in between. It wasn't until I signed a record deal and I start hitting the road that I noticed this "beefy" undercurrent that was starting to swell. And the further I got into my career the more the Christian hip-hip community at large began to grow, and therefore the subsequent division became more pronounced.

The perception of me to many was that I was a youth group rapper. Some said I only became successful because I was white. Others called me an Eminem clone. And some would say I used to be underground and legit, but that I sold out to get the CCM money. I mean, whatever the complaint was against me, back then in 2004/2005 I could see it happen in real-time because of the internet. I explain this because it gives context to a new era and attitude shift I witnessed, first-hand. People became bolder about dissing other people publicly around that time in general, in the culture.

When "Dear Slim" hit, guys started writing songs about me to express their disdain for me. I don't need to name names because it has been quite awhile since this went down. It was interesting because guys that were acquaintances or even friends were all of a sudden literally writing tracks about me, and not in a good way. And they were being bold enough to just take shots at me. This was across the board in the industry; I can't even say it was one type or category of rapper. The black MCs, the white MCs, the Hispanic MCs, the theology cats, the non-theology cats…many of them lined up. I am not going as far to say it was every MC in the scene, but it was enough that it forced to me get Biblical in my response to all of them.

Scripture is kind of clear, if you break it down; if someone sins against you, it says you need to go to them, man-to-man, and discuss it with him. I knew this from my days of being a youth pastor. I knew this from my days of just reading scripture. It never makes sense for anyone to just write a diss track and throw it out into the ether. If you do, everybody starts organizing by tribes and it becomes like a junior-high fist-fight breaking out in the cafeteria. Everyone gathers around yelling, fight, fight, fight, fight. I knew in that moment I had two choices, because I had watched groups like The Tunnel Rats and T Bone go on wax and diss each other back and forth, all throughout the 90's. So, I made a vow and said, if I ever have a national spotlight, I'm not going to repeat the same mistakes.

I decided I had to go track each person down who said something negative about me in public…get a number, get an email, reach out, and talk to them on the phone. I knew, scripturally, that if I felt like I had been disrespected, it was on me to pull them aside and confront them. So, I did this many times. I found that nine times out of ten it usually was enough to calm things down. And, nine times out of ten it turned out to be a simple misunderstanding.

Even though I try to get along with everyone, I'm not the type to run from confrontation. If you want to bring it, then I'm ready to go. I don't mean that in an aggressive way, either. I just mean I will be Biblical in my approach, but I will also be assertive. So a lot of times I would just say, what's your Biblical basis for doing this? And they never usually had one. Usually, a guy would voice a complaint. I would respond with, OK, that's fine. Why didn't you come and talk to me about that? What did you accomplish by writing this song and riling everybody up? That line that you said, that was not even accurate. You're making something up that doesn't even exist that you could have just asked me about.

Usually these conversations began with heat and aggression, but I always made it a point to at least end it with us praying together, which usually meant I was the only one who prayed. But either way, the point was, I knew by handling it that way, I was doing it God's way. And, I was putting out the fire before it even started. And I can tell you that almost every time, after the dust settled, nearly all of them came back to me and apologized.

It's so interesting when you do things God's way it says you can actually win back a brother. And that's usually what happened, even though it was really hard to take it on the chin and resist banging back publicly, either online or in a song. I believe God blessed my career because of all this, and the majority of those people are gone now. And I don't mean that I'm still here because I did things the right way in the prideful sense. The Bible says…who has arguments and fights and bloodshot eyes? It's this type of person you read about often in Proverbs. It's the fool who behaves this way, and it catches up with you, eventually. This is such a small industry. You can't keep setting fire to every bridge you have to walk across. Building bridges with people is what keeps you going.

The beef over "Dear Slim" with other rappers might have died down in the early 2000's for me, but other beefs ensued. Along the way I had issues with journalists who wrote negative things about me. I have had incidents with Calvinists who went after me over being too "wishy-washy" in my lyrics or faith. It has never really stopped, even up until a couple of weeks ago, as of this writing.

But just learning the principal-to go, man-to-man, to someone when you feel wronged by what they said-has saved me so much heartache. It has actually even helped me keep so many great relationships.

The truth is, when you do things God's way, it may not feel great on the front end, but you definitely win on the backend.

CHAPTER 19
JESUS FREAK

TAKEN MOMENTS AFTER WE GOT DONE

"Saw a man with a tat on his big fat belly..." Toby Mack (Jesus Freak)

Soundtrack to this chapter: Jesus Freak ft. Kj52 (newsboys version)

I've had a very interesting relationship with the guys from DC talk over the years. When I first became a Christian, it was also when I first heard of Christian hip hop and simultaneously when I first heard about the group. I remember looking at the two white guys and the black guy and thinking, things are so different in the church world. I'll bet one of the white guys is the rapper and the black guy is the singer. Sure enough, that was exactly what the situation was. I don't mention this to take anything away from their music. On many levels, they pioneered so much in this genre. But those first couple of DC talk albums were just too pop for my tastes. Remember, I came up on militant black hip hop.

It wasn't until the "Free at Last" album that I came around and started listening to DC Talk.

In my opinion, that is one of the most well-produced albums, and I don't mean simply in terms of Christian music. The production value alone is phenomenal for any genre, period. That album really won me over.

Flash-forward to the 90s. Jesus Freak came out and I heard the title track. Immediately, I knew the song was going to be massive. It was the perfect blend of what grunge was and rap was and rock was, but yet so unabashedly Christian at the same time. And I thought, man, someday I want to write a song that perfect. Now at the time I didn't know any of the guys in DC Talk, I didn't even spend much time with Toby, even though I almost signed to Gotee records, his record label. I eventually ended up on Essential Records.

The label actually told me, when my album was finished, that they wanted me to go back into the studio to record a cover of a DC Talk song. The thinking at the time was, they could not identify a clear-cut single on my album, so this would be a way to ensure they had a song that would get play on video shows and radio.

I thought to myself, How in the world am I going to do this? This makes no make sense. But the label was persistent. So, I went back to the Free at Last album and I re-recorded a song titled "The Hard Way." To be honest, I absolutely loved that track, and it was actually Toby Mac himself who fought for that song to be on my album. He stood against his own record label to allow my label to release it.

I have always had a tremendous respect for him as a visionary, as a pioneer, and as someone from the culture. But I never really had a deep connection with him. It was always love, and he always took the time to share advice with me, but I never really knew him in a personal way.

Now, some time later I was on Winter Jam with Michael Tait, in 2002. I shared a tour bus with him, and discovered he was absolutely crazy (in a good way). He cracked me up constantly. He scolded me an entire day one time for eating his ice cream sandwiches, which was an accident on my part, then wound up giving me a whole box for "chastising" me. He was one of the funniest, nicest, most sporadic guys I had ever met. Out of that friendship, every night I would perform "Jesus Freak" and rap the Toby part with Tait (he had just gone solo at the time).

Jump ahead about eight or nine years. I received a random phone call asking if I could be on a plane the following day. They said, don't tell anybody, but we need somebody to redo Toby's part on Jesus Freak with Tait, who's now with the Newsboys. You can't tell anyone. You're going to be on a plane in the morning and you're going to get off. You're going to record it, you're going to get back on the plane and you can't tell a single person. It was nuts. I was going to be a part of the biggest song in Christian music history, and I couldn't tell anybody. And even more bizarre, the guy that was in DC Talk is now in a completely different band and I was going to cover Toby's part. I thought it was the weirdest, best, and the craziest idea all at the same time. Of course, I said yes.

THIS CARDBOARD CUT OUT WAS IN THE STUDIO... I HAD TO GET A PIC.

By the time I hit the plane to go home, people were already texting me to congratulate me. Todd Collins had posted up a pic and had leaked the information and that was it. It was over. The weirdest thing about the whole thing was the fact it was right before I was about to do Winter Jam. On that tour, I was going to be onstage every night with the Newsboys performing Toby's part. At the time Winter Jam became the biggest tour in the country.

The whole experience started to make me realize how little people pay attention. I would come out and do Toby's part, then I would start to watch the Facebook comments. They would say things like, Did you see when Toby came dressed up like KJ to come out on the Newsboys song to do his own part? The song was so big that people could mistake me for being someone else and not even notice. People actually thought that I was Toby at one point. Guys were coming up to me at some of these tour dates and say, man, I've been listening to you since you were in DC talk. And I would literally stand underneath my own banner, which had my name on it, and explain to them I was still in high school when DC Talk came out. There was no way I could be Toby. Still, no one would listen. That's how big that song was…some people didn't even know who actually sang it.

All of it put me in an odd place where I was reaping all the benefits of performing this huge song. Doors were opening up. I was playing big festivals. I was on Winter jam really just to do that part in arenas all across the country in different cities.

The most hilarious moment of it all was when I was booked to be the host at a festival. Toby and Tait were both on the festival, so everyone in the crowd didn't even know I was there. They were thinking Toby was going to come out with The Newsboys to do his part with Tait. Instead, Tait came up to me and said, you're doing the part. Toby wasn't doing it. And I was thinking, this is the most bizarre moment of my life. I'm about to do Toby's part in front of Toby with Tait, who's now with The Newsboys and nobody in the crowd knows that I'm even there.

So, they were all expecting Toby to come out. Right before I was about to go on, I went over to Toby and I just said, "Look man, this is really weird to be doing this in front of you."

He said to me, "No, I wouldn't rather have anyone else do it than you."

And then Gabe, who's one of his guys on stage said, "Yeah, but don't suck."

The song played, I ran out, the crowd went nuts and then literally stopped jumping because they realized it was me and not Toby. They didn't even know how to react. But then they kind of started to realize it was me and got back into it. It was awkward and awesome all at once.

Flash forward about another year and I was at Camp Electric, which is Toby's music camp. I was hosting and Toby had his own part of the evening every night. It was the end of one of the nights and I was exhausted. I was laying in the back of the room slowly starting to nod off. I was really just waiting for the night to get over so I could dismiss the kids, and all of a sudden I hear, KJ get out here! coming from the stage. Toby was asking me to come out for "Jesus Freak" to do his own part.

I was thinking, this makes no sense whatsoever.

In the moment, I actually thought he wanted me to come out and just be a hype man, which I would have been totally fine with. But the song started playing, it arrives at his part, and he just stopped and stepped to the side for me to come in. I'm thinking, this is going to break the time-space continuum. I was performing Toby's part with Toby, even though I've done it with the Newsboys with Toby's former partner, which all goes back to DC talk, which took me back to high school, when that record came out. I mean, it just couldn't get any weirder.

But, I was wrong. It got weirder.

As I was performing I realized I was blanking out on the second verse. Every time I went out with Tait, I only performed the first verse. So, the second verse was about to start and I was about to space out in front of all these kids. And just at the last second, I remembered the lyrics and it turned out to be fine. However, sometimes the band would do this part where they would freeze on stage. So it came to that part and I was the only one that froze. I stood there like a mannequin.

And I thought, I've literally seen it all. I walked off the stage, just shook my head . I thought, yeah, I have literally done everything that I could possibly do on my bucket list. That just happened and it was amazing.

CHAPTER 20
BILL COSBY'S BATHROOM

THIS PIC IS FROM THE "DO THE BILL COSBY" MUSIC VIDEO. WE RECREATED THE COSBY SHOW INTRO... I ALSO NEVER DO THE SONG ANYMORE!

"Why is this rug here?" kj52 (on stage @ Get Motivated Seminar)

Soundtrack to this chapter: "Do the Bill Cosby" kj52 ft. George Moss (Dangerous)

For many years now, I have been performing at this annual business event titled Get Motivated Seminars. As a part of the event, I have had the opportunity to share the stage with some of the biggest names in the world. I have opened for George Bush, Jr., Terry Bradshaw, Steve Forbes, and many others. . Just to be clear, it is not officially a Christian event, though many of the people involved are Christians, and there are subtle faith elements to it. It has been an awe-inspiring occasion every single time, even if my role is to simply entertain the crowd for ten minutes during the lunch break. In addition to sharing the spotlight with some gigantic celebrities, I have also been able to walk onto an arena stage and look out at a crowd of 20,000 people many, many times.

My role in these events has been pretty straight-forward. I lead a dance party for ten minutes, while the attendees take a break from the speakers. This culminates with me giving away a vacation package. I have one specific task, which involves sinking or swimming in front of a crowd who has basically never heard of me. The experience has really taught me a lot about what it means to motivate an audience, especially when they don't care who you are, especially when there is no Christian element to fall back on. In addition, it has been a great chance to let my light shine so to speak in an "undercover" way. My DJ and I do nothing that references faith directly, we are simply a positive, family-friendly presence. As a result, so many doors have opened for me to share my faith on a person to person level. Whether it is behind the scenes conversations with staff, or speaking to someone from the crowd, people go to these events looking for inspiration and direction. We are usually the lone Christian performers on this positive, yet secular event, and we are consistently in a position to share our lives in unique ways we wouldn't normally be able to at a church show or Christian festival.

Of all the famous people we have been able to cross paths with, none is more famous than Bill Cosby (this was before his recent troubles). For a period of time, he consistently performed immediately after us at the seminars. And through the event's employees we learned something that few people in public were aware of: He had basically lost most of his eyesight. This made me feel pretty sad when I first heard about it, because after all, this was Cliff Huxtable we were talking about.

At any rate, after performing the event enough times, we began to notice there would always be this mysterious rug on the stage. We always had to set up and perform on top of this thing, and it didn't make any sense. Do you understand? It had no real business being there. So we began to ask the stage crew if we could move it, and the response was always very stern: "No, under no circumstances can the rug be moved. You can jump on it, you can run on it, you can rap on it. But it absolutely cannot be moved."

For the life of us we couldn't figure it out. It became a consistent-albeit somewhat annoying-joke for us. And then, one day, we finally figured it out; it hit us like a ton of bricks. Bill Cosby was on after us at almost every show. How could we have missed it? Of course…

The rug was there to keep Bill Cosby from falling off the stage because he can't see.

It was a marker for him to feel. He knew that when he was speaking, if he hit the edge of the rug he couldn't go any further. Though this is not the ultimate point of the story, it demonstrates how severe his vision loss was. As you will see, this fact played a key role in what I am about to share. Something to keep in mind, though: the story I am about to tell you took place before we figured out the situation with his eyesight.

So, because we always performed before him, we crossed paths with Mr. Cosby often, as I said, as he was waiting offstage preparing to speak, catching our act. So, he was familiar with me. On one occasion, I was catching a red eye flight from Winter Jam cross-country to meet the Get Motivated Seminar in Portland, and I received a text from the seminar staff saying Bill Cosby requested to meet me when I arrived to the event. I flipped, because at the time he was still my childhood hero, a guy I grew up idolizing almost like a second father (again, this was before his recent troubles)

I am thinking, Who gets to meet Cliff Huxtable?

So when I landed I was super, super nervous. I arrived early in the morning in Portland, and I only had a couple of hours before we were scheduled to take the stage. I was super grimy from the overnight flight, and in a huge rush. When I arrived at the venue for the seminar, I was pretty desperate to get cleaned up. And we never had our own green room like all the big wigs; all we had was a little pipe and drape set up on the venue floor. So I snuck in to use one of the bathrooms to shave, mainly because I didn't want to look homeless when I met bill Cosby. Now keep in mind, this was before I knew he had sight issues.

So I went into the bathroom backstage and I start to shave. My DJ was also in there as well. He cleaned himself up, and then he left. So I was all alone in this bathroom we really weren't supposed to be using, technically, because it belonged to someone very important. When my DJ was still in there we actually made a joke....Wouldn't it be hilarious if this was Bill Cosby's bathroom? Then, as I was shaving, I started to hear voices outside the bathroom door. I was terrified because I didn't want to get in trouble. There was no way for me to exit in a subtle way because there was only one door to the bathroom. You have to understand how tight the security was at these events. They didn't play. They had dogs that sniffed for bombs. Secret Service was everywhere. I'm thinking, What if it's Laura Bush's room? What if the Secret Service comes in and arrests me?

So I had no choice. I had no other way out. I just finished shaving and walked out the door like I was supposed to be there. As I did so, I saw the back of somebody's head. It was a black male's head, and I saw one of the staff from our event with the guy. I breathed a sigh of relief, thinking, I am safe, I am not going to Secret Service jail. And then I realized it was Bill Cosby.

No joke, I just used Bill Cosby's bathroom.

So, you have to picture this. I tried to nonchalantly sneak by, so I could slip out the door, then casually walk back in again, to make it seem like I wasn't just in Bill's bathroom. And as I walked by, the seminar staffer says, "Oh, there's the guy you wanted to talk to, right there!."

I was caught. And I will never forget that moment. Bill turned around and looked at me, then around the room, as if I was a ghost floating around, invisible. Like, he couldn't find where I was, even though I was standing right in front of him. And it became clear to me…He's visually impaired. He's basically blind. My first reaction was relief. I mean, he couldn't have actually seen me coming out of his bathroom, because, you know, he's like, blind. He reached out his hand, and I shook it. Then, he said, "You're the Christian rapper guy, aren't you?"

I sat down and said, "Yes, Sir, it's an honor to meet you."

The next thing he did totally blew me away. He immediately launched into a whole speech about how I needed to have my own TV show, and that it needed to be on the WB. No joke. He literally had a very specific plan for my life and career that he had spent time pondering and had been itching to tell me. Of course, I'm thinking, No way my manager is just going to call the WB and get a TV show. It will never happen in a million years. So, I was just sitting there listening to him lay out my life's plan like it is a foregone conclusion I was going to be a big TV star. And I couldn't say anything. It was Bill Cosby. I couldn't just respond with, "No, sorry, thanks for the input, but it's not going to happen."

The whole conversation was over in a matter of moments. Once he finished his speech about my future in Television he put out his hand as an obvious signal that it was time for me to leave. It was surreal. I couldn't even catch up with all the thoughts racing through my head on so many levels. I mean, the whole thing was incredibly awkward… and the vibe he sent me that it was time for me to exit his room immediately was thick. He was basically saying, you may leave my room now, son ,without saying a word.

I was Theo Huxtable in that moment. I had just gotten grounded and asked to go to my room. Do you understand how I felt?

So, I stood up and he put out his hand.
Then he said, "Never forget it's a music…."

And then he just stopped. He didn't say anything.
He wanted me to finish his sentence. After a couple of moments of shock and awe, I responded, "Business."

And he said, "Don't ever forget that."

Then, I just walked out and found my DJ. I said, "I just had the weirdest five-minute conversation with Cliff Huxtable. It was so strange I can't even put it into words."

And THEN, after that, I started having all these subsequent Bill Cosby interactions and strange sightings. For example, he ran into Jamie Grace, who is a CCM artist, in an airport. He just went straight up to her and started talking to her while she was playing her guitar. She told him she was a Christian singer. I had told Jamie the previous story I just mentioned when he spoke to her. So she said, "Oh, I know KJ." And Bill responded by just talking about me like he knew me. They had an entire conversation about me.

Jamie. And, Bill Cosby.

I should also mention that shortly after the first interaction with him, I wrote the song "Do The Bill Cosby," inspired by these events. Then, I ended up running into him again and it was after just coming out of the bathroom again. No joke. My hands were still wet from washing my hands. He was standing there, and I shook his hand.

Then he said, "What is it with you and bathrooms?" A bunch of people were standing around as he said this, and they all just died laughing.

And I said, "I have no answer, Sir."

He said, "Well, I hope that's water on your hands."

So then, I told him about the song I wrote called "Do the Bill Cosby." At that moment it was like I was living some kind of bizarre fantasy that wasn't even my real life.

Now, years later, Bill is in trouble. And I have people texting me left and right. Some are people are saying, "'Do the Bill Cosby' has a whole different meaning now.'" Of course, as soon as I heard the first mention of that controversy I took the song out of my set. I also stopped selling my "Do the Bill Cosby" shirt or performing the song, too. I had to distance myself completely from the whole thing.

The lesson? At the end of the day, people are just people. They are partly good. They are also partly bad. To be more specific, scripture says that we are all fallen. The reality is, the statement "never meet your heroes" is kind of an accurate thought in hindsight. But my takeaway was, whatever your opinion is on the guy, I just found it very interesting that our faith shone through without us even ever really having to open our mouths and speak the message. You know what I mean? The lesson is, you can be a light in the darkness sometimes by not even trying to shine your light overtly or intentionally. Because the light is in you, it will shine naturally, because the world is such a dark place. And again, you never know who you will cross paths with because of it.

Bill Cosby's Bathroom | 97

CHAPTER 21
AGREE TO DISAGREE

- PROBABLY ONE OF THE ONLY CHAPTERS I THOUGHT ABOUT LEAVING OUT MY BOOK BUT ITS SO NECESSARY TO LEARN HOW TO WORK THRU CONFLICT BIBLICALLY..

*'Check this guy.. ain't a bird or plane..
its the God man there ain't no Lois Lane" kj52 (Superhero)*

Soundtrack to this chapter: Superhero KJ52 (dangerous album)

So a little later in my career, I was invited to be a part of something called Fine Arts for the Assemblies of God. It was actually a convention for Assemblies of God ministers from all over the country. I was invited to perform a pre-service set, then actually play another song that had a connection to some of the missions work the AG was doing. This was a pretty big deal because they don't normally invite artists to perform. I just happened to be a former Assemblies of God minister, and I had a really good relationship with a lot of the organizers.. This was a big opportunity, so I didn't want to take it lightly.

I know my denomination well enough to know that there is still a degree of traditionalism. In denominations which are established and have a decent history, there is a tug-of-war between new methods and the old. So I said, "Well, if they invited me, I'm going to do it the way I normally do my show". Honestly, I don't have much secular music in my set, but I do a couple of "fun" songs which aren't necessarily Christian, but do have an intention behind them that is still ministry-focused in the bigger picture of my performance. At the end of the day, music is entertainment, so I am not super rigid about introducing harmless cover material that isn't overtly faith-based, so long as it doesn't distract the audience from the true purpose.

So, I played the pre-show in front of a couple thousand kids. It was an amazing show, no doubt. I went back on just a little bit later. Like I said, this was a special, one-song 'encore" which consisted of a song that I wrote essentially to urge kids to donate to missions and reach the global community. I have to stress to you that I had very honest intentions in what I was doing. The whole show came off without a hitch; The response was phenomenal. I had an amazing time. After the show I left with the memory of what seemed to be a perfect show.

A couple of weeks later, however, I received a text from a friend. He said, "Yo, man, they are destroying you on television.

I replied, "What? What are you talking about?"

He said, "Oh, you're on the Swaggart Network right now. Check it out. They're telling people that you're leading people to hell and what you're doing is demonic. They are saying that everything you're doing is not of God, and that you are one of the reasons why the Assemblies of God has lost its focus."

I kind of took it in stride and didn't take it too seriously. I figured I was a part of some expose' about how all Christian music is evil. I didn't really think too much about it, to be honest. Then, a couple days later I receive another text. And, the person contacting me said Gabe Swaggart (Jimmy Swaggart's grandson) preached an entire sermon about my performance. He said that I was bringing down The Assemblies of God, and that the entire denomination is compromising from top to bottom.

And I thought to myself, this can't be true.

But sure enough, I dug around and found the message. It was titled "The New Cart." The gist of the message was, when they transported the Ark of the Covenant, they put it on a new cart instead of moving it the specific way that God commanded. It was an easier way to move it, and one that was more modern to the people. So, God struck them down because of it. You can see where he was going with this...

I watched the video of the message. And as I got into it, I saw he had edited together short clips of my set to create a narrative that fit the message. Then, he edited some statements from the superintendent of the Assemblies of God right after, which was the moment when he said, "the Lord is in this place". So, in other words, he edited it together to make it look like I performed, and then the highest member of the AG jumped up there and endorsed me. Of course, that is not what happened at all. Actually, the guy didn't come on until like a half an hour later, and had nothing to do with my performance.

Then, he spliced together all the parts of my songs that are secular. There were little snippets of a Prince song, some other songs from the Eighties, and the like. Just to be clear- I have little moments in my set where I reference popular songs that the whole crowd knows in order to engage them, but I always bring it back to the higher purpose involved. As I watched this, my jaw was wide open. It was a forty-five minute sermon about how hip-hop was demonic, and how the Assemblies of God had lost their focus. He was saying they were trying to use new methods to reach kids instead of using the old message, which was the "true" gospel. My performance was being used as an example of this.

A thousand things were going through my head. First, I felt super embarrassed because I felt like I let down the people that had given me the shot to play. Second, I started to feel outraged because they had taken a hatchet to my performance to fit an agenda. Third, I was just upset because I felt like the whole thing was such a twist of scripture. It was a classic example of someone using the Bible for a human motive which was based on a certain traditional mindset.

I had two choices in my response. I could go on the offensive and defend myself. I was about to do just that using any channels at my disposal. I could have posted on the sermon website, for starters, then use my social media, mailing list, whatever. I wanted to defend myself publicly because I had been attacked publicly. Then, I had a conversation with my DJ right before I was going to do it. He said, "There might be a better way to do this."

He was right. So, I found Gabe Swaggart on Twitter and asked him if we could talk privately. I basically said, hey man, I think there might be some misunderstanding about me. I'd love to talk to you one on one.

I didn't do anything publicly. I just went straight to him, man-to-man, as the scripture tells us to in Matthew 18 . People all around me were outraged for me as well, getting all fired up. There were more than a few people telling me I deserved to bang back in public eye.

To my surprise, Gabe hit me back pretty quickly, and we jumped on the phone. Now, his persona in the sermon was very fire and brimstone. But, when I got on the phone with him, he was super cordial and willing to dialog. I said, "Let's just reason with each other from the scriptures. I could defend myself, but let's allow the Bible to guide the conversation."

I started by referencing the verses where Paul talks about becoming all things to all men to reach some. Then, I also mentioned scriptures where Paul quoted from the secular poetry of his day. Then, I asked Gabe what his take was on it. I said, do you know that he's quoting from pagan secular sources to prove a point? He wasn't hearing me. We went back and forth for about forty-five minutes. His point was that rap music came from the influence of Voodoo drums. He said rap music has its roots in African pagan music, and therefore it is demonic. I reminded him that his great uncle was Jerry Lee Lewis, and that was a similar music style to the music his grandfather embraced. I made the point that Jimmy Swaggart's music was basically the same music and that there is no demonic beat. I said, So, if you are telling me a four-four beat (which is the basic beat of all hip-hop music) is demonic, then we're all in trouble, aren't we?

There wasn't really any way to reason with him with scriptures. What it came down to was that he preached the message God laid on his heart. He just kept saying that. This is what God laid on my heart. So you can't really argue against that, whenever anyone says that. That can be interpreted as code for who are you to question (what God has given me) God? It's always the end of the discussion when someone claims God is speaking through them.

I couldn't control his opinion of me or what I do, in the end. All I could do was respond to him thoughtfully and carefully, in as Godly and respectfully of a way as possible. I walked him through the scriptural basis for why I do what I do. I tried to make him see where he was doing the same thing, but where he was changing the meaning of the verses to fit what he was trying to convey. We had to agree to disagree by the end of the conversation.

But I did ask him if I could pray for him when we finished. I asked him if he still thought I was demonic when I did so. He said yes, but still prayed with me anyway. There was a part of me that still was frustrated when it was over, of course. Part of me still wanted to go on the offensive. There was also still a part of me that felt like I had really let down the denomination that had helped my faith so much.

Just after that, I started getting all this support from the very highest level of the assemblies of God. People had seen me send Gabe a Twitter message asking him to speak privately, but they also saw I didn't say anything else publicly. One person said thank you for handling the situation biblically. Another said thank you for not returning evil for evil. Still another thanked me and said, we believe in you.

I kept Gabe's number, and we kept in touch via text here and there. One time, just to be funny, I took a picture of a shopping cart and said, look, it's my new cart. It actually became a friendly relationship. For many years, I was not sure if his viewpoint had evolved. Years later, I actually reconnected with him when I began to write this story, and we actually found that we agreed on more than we disagreed on. I feel like time, understanding, and prayer actually helped to heal the sore that was there between us. All I do know is that I was able to handle it biblically, and I didn't go on the offensive. I didn't compromise or fire back.

God taught me that Gabe is my brother in Christ. I learned whether or not you see eye to eye with someone, you can still deal with each other in a manner that is respectful and grace-filled. I also learned we have to look at the examples in scripture where two people disagree. In those situations, the best thing to do is to pull the person aside and try to work it out privately. If you can't find common ground, you have to let it go.

And the truth of the matter is, if I wanted to text him right now, I could, and I know he would hit me right back… even if I do have a new cart.

CHAPTER 22
GUINNESS WORLD RECORD HOLDER

ORIGINAL FLYER

"I don't want to ever do that again..." kj52 (after 13 hours of freestyling)

Soundtrack to this chapter: TROY instrumental (the first beat we rhymed to when we started)

Five or six years ago, a good friend of mine who has now since passed, was diagnosed with a debilitating cancer. His name was DJ Official. I had known him for quite awhile, and I didn't feel like I could just sit by and do nothing while his medical bills mounted. So, I was trying to think of creative ways that I could raise money for him. I kicked around a bunch of ideas but landed on the notion of doing a freestyle rap marathon. Meaning, people could sponsor us by the minute or by the hour, and all the money could go towards his medical bills. Before I ever thought about setting a world record for freestyling I thought I would put my gifts and talents to good use by giving the money to DJ Official.

In the process of doing all this, Lecrae, who had a massive social media following, put out a tweet and basically paid his bills in two days. So, it wound up being unnecessary for me to host a freestyle marathon because the money was already raised. But in the process of it I wondered if a Guinness world record existed for freestyling. I started doing some research, and I came to find there were two categories to compete in, there was an individual category and there was also a team category. I figured the team one would be a doable shot considering I had a few really great freestylers in my immediate circle.

I didn't really want to do the individual freestyle category, because I couldn't imagine rhyming for fourteen hours straight. But I thought the team record was attainable, because it was only seven or eight hours long. At the time I knew four or five really good freestyle hip-hop artists locally who were believers. So, I thought "We might be able to actually do this!". If we could get five people together, and if all of us could freestyle for an hour by ourselves, then all of us freestyled together as a team for an hour and we kept repeating that angle, that would be ten hours right there.

So I sent in an application, and immediately the application was approved! At the time I was hitting a rock bottom point in my career where many things I had been counting on to happen, didn't. I started thinking about what sort of legacy I was going to leave if I had to exit the industry that year. If I was going to quit, right then, had I checked off all my bucket list items? Had I done everything I thought I was going to do? These were the questions I was asking myself. I thought about the fact that no one in Christian hip-hop had a world record for anything.

So, I started to assemble a dream team of sorts, which included two guys from a group called Free Daps (Issac Knox and Heir Jordan). I also lined up a female by the name of Sicily, and another guy named Jerell Johnson. The five of us could hold it down for an hour each, no problem. I contacted them and I asked if they were down, and they all said yes, emphatically.

I had the team, but I didn't yet have a venue. The weird thing was, the list of rules and verifications that I had to do for Guinness was a mile long. It was going to be a pile of administrative work to pull off. It was actually more work to verify the record than to actually set the record. So, I kicked around the idea some more, then I reached out to my good friend Tommy Kylonnen of Crossover Church. His place had been a hip-hop church for years, way before it was cool to have a hip-hop church. Of all the places to do this thing, Crossover was the place to do it.

The church was in Tampa, about two hours away from me. It was literally in the Toys R' Us building where I used to buy my GI Joe's as a child. After talking with him, he said we should do it on a Sunday, simultaneously along with the church service. The idea being that when we were about to break the record, we could actually end the evening service. We could freestyle live for everyone in attendance as we broke it literally bookending the day around Sunday AM and PM services.

I realized this was the perfect situation with the benefit of a church and volunteers to help verify everything as well as live streaming by the website Jam the hype. They had built in technology, which would be able to do all the video recording we needed for Guinness along with allowing us to take freestyle topics from a live chat room. Everything lined up incredibly well, and I realized that we had a really good shot at breaking the world record.

As we began to put the whole thing together, I began to think we shouldn't just rap for twelve hours straight, that would have been crazy boring. I thought we were all too creative to stick to that basic plan. So the idea was that each one of us would approach our own verse the way we each wanted to and we would approach our team hour by playing freestyle games. We were going to do improv, essentially. At one point we played a game called headbands, during which we had to guess the topic that was on your own headband all the while freestyling for clues.

HEADBANDS RULES!

I mean, we really took freestyling to the level of Improv theater on many levels.

I knew I wanted to surround myself with people who were going to inspire me when it came time to do my hour. So, I brought up my drummer, hypeman and a phenomenal beatboxer named Rubox. We also had a DJ at one point for several of the sets.

I had every one I wanted assembled to inspire me, but the most important person there was my rhyme partner from when I was fourteen years old, Greg. He came during my hour and played upright, standup bass the whole time. It was something we couldn't help but laugh about as we looked at each other. We would have never dreamed when we were fourteen that someday we would break a world record together for freestyling.

I should mention, the biggest reason why I wanted to do it as a team was to ensure no one of us could ever take credit for any of it. Meaning, it was a team effort. And I thought it really depicted what the body of Christ was and is supposed to be about. This was the difference between Christian hip-hop and mainstream hip-hop. If I broke the record myself, I would have gotten all the glory, but if we did it together, God would receive the glory.

MY MAN GREG ON THE UPRIGHT BASS!

About thirty minutes in, I started realizing it was going to be one of the hardest things I had ever done. The amount of mental, physical and spiritual exhaustion was like nothing I had ever dealt with. Freestyling requires so much brain capacity. It pushed me to the limit of everything I was. We were only allowed to have 5 minute mandated breaks each hour and if we were to pause longer than 3 seconds in the freestyle the entire attempt would have been nullified.

I thought, in the moment, that the whole thing represented the way the body of Christ is supposed to work. When you get tired out, someone else is there to step in and help you and hold your arms up…just like they did with Moses.

We did it. Ten hours into it, we broke the record.

Many people reached out beforehand and wanted to be a part of the world record attempt. I asked them each to send me a video of their freestyle for thirty minutes to an hour, but nobody did. So there was no way I could entrust any of the "applicants" to handle it. But, the true beauty of the record category was that anybody's name could be put on it as long as they rapped for at least five minutes. So, once we broke the record at ten hours, we opened up the mic for anyone to jump on.

So, while it was a core team of five that did it, we added like another twenty (or so) people at the end. That's why we were actually able to go for twelve hours and two minutes in the end. When it was all said and done, there wasn't one person that walked away with the props.

God received all the glory, and here we are, all these years later, and we still hold the record.

NAILED IT!

CHAPTER 23
MARY vs MARTHA

I DON'T KNOW WHY I LOOK TO THE SIDE SO OFTEN IN MY PROMO PICS...

"Remember... Grandmas like hip hop, too"
~ Godspeed from Grandma Patti

Soundtrack to this chapter: More of You Less of Me (Jonah LP)

A couple of years ago, I released my first independent album titled Jonah. At that time, I had just unofficially joined the staff at my church, as well. It was a very busy time. So, there were a thousand things going through my head, because the church was hosting my album release party, and we were also launching a young adult ministry. It's amazing how you can get caught up in all the busyness of ministry and lose sight of actual, real-life opportunities to reach people in a deeper way, interpersonally. This episode was one such case, I almost missed out on an amazing chance to directly help someone.

Like I said, that moment in time for me was the culmination of a ton of hard work to release my first album independently. I had financed the whole thing strictly through crowdfunding, utilizing donations from my core fanbase . I was taking on most of the responsibilities of the release by myself, whereas in the past I had a label and a team to handle most of the admin with my previous records. I learned it is a ridiculous amount of work to release your work independently.

IM REALLY PROUD OF THIS ALBUM FOR MANY REASONS.

This was a really big turning point for me because a year or so prior I was ready to quit. A career reinvention was happening before my eyes, culminating in this night, my album release show. Again, I was definitely busy with all day-to-day work, especially on that day. I had a big night in front of me and I was lost in the details…setting up, preparing for the show, etc.

And I'll never forget, the first CD I ever sold that night was to a sweet, retiree lady. She must have been in her seventies or eighties. She just walked into the church, headed straight to my table and said she wanted to buy a record. I was a little confused, so I informed her that the music was rap. She said she knew that and she loved my music and what I was all about.

It was such an ironic moment, selling my first independent disc to an elderly woman. I reflected on it then and there for a few minutes, quietly. The whole scene reminded me of the Martha versus Mary moment, one of these women sat down to learn while the other one was busy doing things for Jesus. Anytime you are involved in ministry you can find yourself in the same situation. In other words, you can spend tons of time doing things for Jesus and not spend any time actually with him. If you don't know what I mean yet, read on.

Minutes later, this random kid walked in off the street. He was looking around, seeming lost. He had a look on his face like he just needed to talk to somebody. And in a moment I thought, I'll refer him to one of the pastors. The last thing I need to do right now is counseling with some kid over some issue that he's probably had problems with a thousand times. After all, he could be a crazy person. After all, I had so much to do, so much going on, and I wasn't technically even a pastor on staff. But, then he said, "I just was wondering if I could come in and pray."

So I told him to go right in to the sanctuary if you want to pray, go for it. He walked into the big, empty room and sat down, alone. And I went back to just setting up my merchandise. Then, something hit me. It was as if the voice of God rose above all the noise in that moment and reminded me, you are doing all these things for me, but what are you actually doing? That's my heart, that kid in there.

So I walked into the sanctuary. It was dead quiet. There was nobody else there. I sat down and I said, "Hey man, you seem distraught. Are you okay? Is there anything I can help you with?"

He just looked up at me and said, "I don't know how to pray and I want to give my life to God."

In that moment I thought, man, I would have missed this because I was so busy doing my "Christian rap ministry." I was so busy setting up for my big release show that I almost forgot why I was doing it all in the first place. At the end of the day, it is still about people. This kid was why I do what I do, and I came so close to passing up the opportunity! All I ever wanted to do was just reach people. Not necessarily the masses, but primarily individuals.

So, I talked with him and I listened to him. And I asked, "Have you ever read the Bible?"

He said, "No."

I said, "Well, can I just share some verses with you?" And I just walked him through what it meant to surrender your life to Christ.

After I finished explaining the basics of salvation to him, such as how all of us are guilty before a Holy God. I opened the book of Romans and began to walk him through multiple verses and then I asked, "Do you understand what these things mean?"

He said, "Yeah."

I said, "Do you understand that without Christ you're lost and there's a penalty for your mistakes?"

And he responded, "Yeah, I understand."

I said, "Do you understand now God is asking what you will do with that? Are you willing to turn from your life and to give everything to Him?"

He responded, "Yeah, I want to."

So, I said, "Can I lead you in a prayer to do that?"

And right there in that moment we prayed. Then, he looked up and he said the same exact thing I said the day after I gave my life to Christ.
He said, "Something feels different."

I gave Him some information about the church and how he could continue to grow. Then, I said, "Okay man, God bless you. I'll be praying for you." And just like he came in, I more or less turned around and he disappeared. It was just that fast. I never saw him again.

It was such a gut check. It was as if God was asking me directly, What are you doing this for 20 years later? You're still at it, but what are you actually doing it for? Are you doing it so you can sell some merch and CDs? Are you just here to play for a packed crowd and feel like the man, or is it still about people? Is it still about people that are hurting, who need to know there is an answer?

It wasn't an accident that he came in when he did. He was no different than I was when I was fifteen. It was a reminder, directly from above.

CHAPTER 24
Q & A + QUOTES

SOMEDAY I'll AFFORD PANTS W/O HOLES

I love lists and quotes, I make myself a to do list everyday and built a career off of punchlines. Some of this stuff didn't really warrant its own story/chapter but this will give you some insight into this odd brain that I have along with some quotes from people close to me.

Biggest shows ever played?
- Marrakech Morocco 50k +
- Georgia Dome Get Motivated 25k+
- Flevo Festival (Amsterdam) 25k+

k + MUSLIMS IN THIS PIC

Favorite Food?
- Mediterranean
- Cuban/Puerto Rican/Jamaican
- Street Tacos
- Cheesecake
- Chic-fil-A
- Snobby Pour Over Coffee

Awkward Fan Moments?
- My neighbor who stalked me online (we're good friends with the fam now ha ha).
- The guy in the gym bathroom who tried to lead me to Christ with my own music because "I looked like kj52".
- Two girls that came to my house to invite me to come speak at their church that night.
- The girl that was staring at me when I woke up in the middle of the night on a redeye flight then told me "I'm a big fan..".
- The girl who was my bench press partner (long story.. total accident) and revealed she was a fan when the bar was on my chest.
- The nurse that was helping deliver my first kid who broke down crying when she revealed my music really helped her kid.

Who are some people you've been told you look like?
- Rob Dyrdek
- Tony Romo
- Liam Neeson
- Kevin Spacey
- Temoh Gonzalez (mariachi singer)
- Ad• Rock from The Beastie Boys

Top Sneakers?
- Air Max 92 & 95
- Air Jordan IV
- Converse Chuck Taylors
- British Knights
- Air Force 1's
- Checkerboard Van's
- Nike Cortez

Favorite Sports Teams?
- Tampa Bay Bucs (Superbowl era)
- Miami Hurricanes (late 80's-mid 90s era)
- Michigan Wolverines (Desmond Howard era)
- Detroit Pistons (hammer time era)
- Detroit Tigers (late 80s)

STILL LOVE THE 'CANES!

Favorite TV Shows?
- The Office
- Seinfeld
- The Walking Dead
- X-Files

Favorite Movies?
- The Breakfast Club
- Ferris Bueller's Day Off
- Empire Strikes Back
- The Matrix
- Napoleon Dynamite
- Do The Right Thing

Favorite Documentaries?
- Style Wars
- Exit Through the Gift Shop
- 30 for 30 (Miami Hurricanes)
- Beats, Rhymes and Life (A Tribe Called Quest doc)

Favorite Bands/Artists/Albums/Songs?
- The Police (Best of)
- Mutemath (Mutemath)
- Phil Collins (Best of)
- The Cure (Boys Don't Cry)
- The Smiths (Please, Please, Please)
- Talking Heads (Once in a Lifetime)
- INXS (Kick)
- U2 (Joshua Tree)
- Hall & Oates (I can't go for that)
- Prince (Purple Rain)
- Steely Dan (Peg)

Favorite Producers?
- Timbaland
- Neptunes
- Dr. Dre
- Pete Rock
- DJ Premier
- Todd Collins
- Goldinchild

Favorite Rap Groups?
- Public Enemy (Fear of Black Planet)
- 3rd Bass (the Cactus)
- A Tribe Called Quest (Best of)
- De La Soul (3 ft. High and Rising)
- Beastie Boys (Pauls Boutique)

Favorite Rappers?
- Nas
- Common
- Rakim
- KRS ONE

Favorite CHH artists?
- SFC (Illumination)
- PID (Chosen Ones)
- LPG (The Earthworm)
- Freedom of Soul (The Second Comin')
- Grits (Art of Translation)

Favorite Graff Writers/Street Artists?
- Keo xmen
- Zephyr
- Seen
- Camer1
- Banksy

Favorite Bible Verse?
- Proverbs 18:24

Favorite Cities/Towns to visit/play?
- NY
- Miami
- Seattle
- LA
- Detroit
- Higgins Lake MI
- YBOR CITY
- Orlando
- Toronto

Favorite Comic Books?
- Wolverine
- Batman
- Superman
- Dark Horse Comics (Alien vs Predator series)
- Aquaman
- Elf Quest
- G.I. Joe

Best things you ever did?
- got saved
- got married
- had kids
- got healthy
- got organized
- got efficient
- got into community
- got accountable
- never stopped learning
- walked in forgiveness daily

Favorite Albums you did?
- Jonah
- Sons of Intellect
- Yearbook
- Collaborations

Favorite Song you did?
- Whatever the last one is that I worked on.

Favorite Cartoons?
- Robotech
- Transformers
- G.I. Joe
- Voltron
- Gforce
- Star Raiders

Top Books you've read?
- Where the Sidewalk Wnds
- Everything You Need To Know About The Music Business
- ADHD: A New Perception
- Beastie Boys Book
- Just For Kicks
- Subway Art
- Wild at Heart
- Every Mans Battle
- Autobiography of Malcom X

What are some things people may not know about you?
- I have tinnitus in my right ear.
- I've had two concussions.
- My broken nose never healed properly so the cartilage in my nose isn't straight.
- I have bad vision.
- I was in a Kool-Aid commercial.
- My first kiss was 10 years old... first real kiss was at 13.
- I have a hard time falling asleep most nights.
- I have all my wisdom teeth.
- I was in gifted classes most of my early schooling.
- I lived in Ireland for two months & spent an entire summer in Idaho.
- The only places I haven't played are South America, Asia & Antartica.
- I'm constantly tapping out a rhythm or moving to a beat.
- I write couplets of verses/topics/choruses and punchline phrases all the time.
- I've worked as a bottle boy/flower delivery man/phone survey/census worker and a waiter.
- I have light sensitive eyes so I have to wear shades outside.
- I rarely sunburn.
- I'm Sicilian/Slovakian/Irish/Scottish & probably some other stuff I don't know...
- I was born in Miami grew up in the Tampa area and moved to SWFL when I was 15.

If you just hopped off of a time machine circa 1995ish and could share one piece of wisdom with young Jonah…what would it be?
(submitted via kickstarter by Devin)
- I probably could just copy and paste the 3rd verse from my "Hold On" song from the Jonah album (cause thats basically who I was talking to) but I would just say take the time to enjoy the moment. I would tell myself that it does get easier, your dreams will come true... learn to listen more and speak less and passionately go after your gift and calling. I'd also tell myself to start working out now so you don't get overweight at 27... (mt. dew and cheeseburgers are a killer).

(cont. • • >)

What advice would you give to the teens of today regarding the ways of the world? (How to avoid the deceptions that are built into this world)
-*Sherry (who I used to sing "holiday road" with all the time at my first job in Higgins Lake)*
• I think its super important to establish a group around you that can hold you accountable and/or provide a positive influence on your life. We should be thermostats not thermometers, simply because thermostats set the temperature while thermometers just read the temperature (stole this from Pastor Cory Demmel). You can either go along with everyone or you can set the pace. That is the one thing that has guided my life ever since I came to Jesus at 15.

"Your lyrics in your songs are some of the most impactful and thought‑provoking that I've heard in music, and I've always loved your unique ability to look at Christianity in new perspectives. For example, songs like "Life After Death," "Cry No More," "What If" "Sonshine," "5th Element," etc. Is there any good story or inspiration you have behind any of those songs, that you could share?
(Talon Diwisch from Canada)
• This is is a great question! I've always sought to take concepts that we get desensitized to (such as biblical truth) and shine a new perspective on it. It usually begins with the process of writing down ideas, concepts, lyric starters and/or stuff that God is showing me in His word. I tend to draw inspiration from my own life and combine it with a biblical worldview to come up with a new perspective on it. I was just always raised to look at things from multiple angles, my hope is always to catch people a little off guard so I can get them to look at God's truth in a new way.

"I've been a fan of KJ for about 12 years now. I came across his music when a youth group leader of mine introduced me to the Yearbook cd. At that time I didn't know there was such thing as christian rap and I was very new in my faith. I found myself immersed in everything that KJ had from his Podcast to his music videos to his cds and his concerts, I had finally found someone who was not only just a Godly man but also who did rap music, I thought that was pretty cool. KJ became like a best friend to me, my parents always heard his music playing in my room and they would always hear him on his Podcast. His music was always there for me, he was always there for me. When I was in the toughest spots and when my faith was weak I would put on a KJ cd and I would be reminded of God's great glory, who god is and what he can do in my life. God used KJ in my life to not only strengthen my faith but show me that life can be fun and exciting, full of laughs and full of Gods goodness and also show me who God is and how he can change my life.
Thank you KJ" *- Ian Jones*

"The first time I met Jonah, I punched him in the stomach and we've been friends ever since. What often goes unnoticed in his immense humor is the amount of depth and transparency that has made Jonah a cornerstone of musical voices in the Christian Music space. It's only natural his book would reflect those amazing qualities."
- **Derek Minor**

(who's son once hugged my leg and said "Daddy it's a MAN!" and it was pretty much the best hug ever)

MY MAN DEREK

"Jonah and I share the same zany (non) sense of humor which, over the years, has led to many belly laughs, sore sides, inside jokes and even our own language." - **Bryan Stapp**

(who used to jab me in the side during church and throw wet socks at my face to wake me up when I lived with his family)

— THIS WAS FROM GRADUATION DAY, ALL I REMEMBER IS THAT IT DOWNPOURED ON US AND MY HAT MELTED.

CHAPTER 25
CONCLUSION

I hate goodbyes so I'll try to make them as quick as possible. Not sure why that is, I just have a hard time saying "peace" to the ones I love. I find its easier to either just not say it, or get it over as quickly as I can. So rather than saying goodbye I'd like to say thank you for spending time with me through this story telling session.

Thank you for all your support.

This latest incarnation of my career has been a tough one. In a weird way I'm doing exactly what I've prayed for and it's been the hardest 5 years of my life. I've had more broken relationships happen, more money lost and more rock bottom situations than I care to elaborate on.

Conversely, the highs have been massive.. I've seen things that I've only dreamed of become a reality. I suppose the two things can't exist without the other, I know that God is doing it all for a reason. I have to trust in that.

I don't know exactly what the future holds but I do know who holds the future. I know He'll be leading the way just like He did for each and everyone of these stories that I told in this book. I'm going to end this book with the same thing I just said to someone as I was leaving...

"I love you, I appreciate you and I pray you have an amazing everything.."

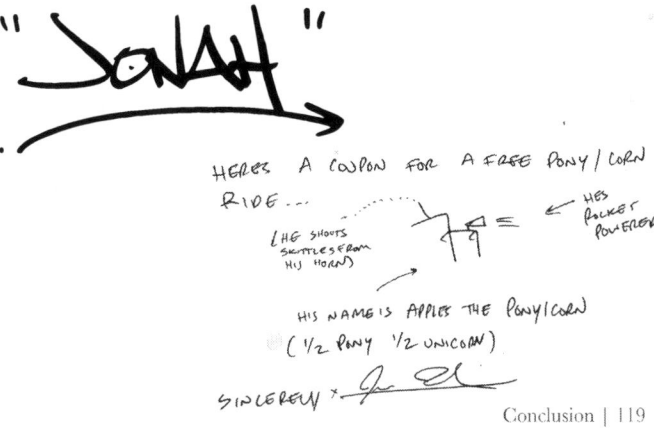

GALLERY

One of my favorite shots of us when I was 20 and she was 22.

My aunt bonnie used to throw me and cousin in the car and just take off into the florida swampland on an "adventure" .. she snapped a pic of me in my usual "hamming it up" pose.

Me and my cousin (who was like my brother growing up cuz i was an only child till 10) ... i still do this dumb look on my face by default when i take pics... don't ask me why.

Modeling shot when I was 7, I insisted on wearing camo because I was obsessed with G.I. Joe.

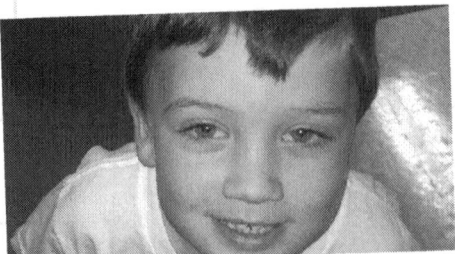

My middle son Zay.

Poppa dukes.. sometime around mid 80's.

One of my first shows, don't ask me why I have a Kansas jersey on.. I certainly had never been to Kansas at that time.

Bible college visit my senior year, the night prior they called security on me for doing that "Shaka Zulu rap stuff" and told me I'd never do that on that campus... years later I headlined a show at that school.

Modeling headshots... buck teeth and all.

My oldest song shooting his bubble gun at me.

My mom holding me and my cousin as babies.

My parents and aunt lounging sometime in 76-77 I would assume.

Higgins Lake.. trying super hard to get Amy to like me.. I grabbed her hair clip and was rocking it as a bow tie with a Pee Wee Herman voice... lets just say it didnt work.

One of my favorite pics of my wife that I snapped when she was lost in thought.. I've painted this image a few times and its still my phone screen saver.

My youngest son.

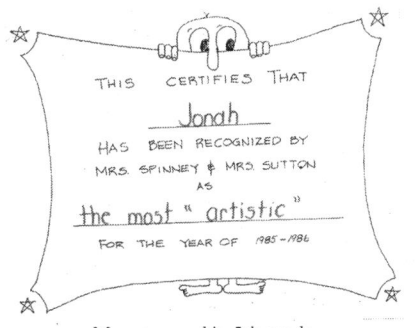

My art award in 5th grade.

5th grade note from my teachers.

A list of song concepts for my collaborations album, notice the "Dear Slim" one.

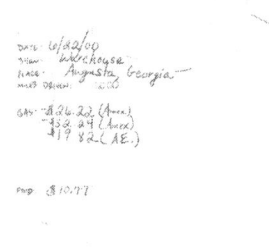

First show on my first tour I played for 5 people and made $45 dollars.

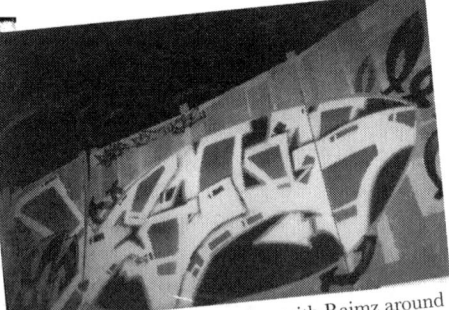

Collaborative ichthus fish piece with Raimz around 2002 I think.. I was starting to get better @ graff untill I hit the road pretty hardcore and didnt have time to keep practicing.

I lived in Ireland with my mom/aunt and cousins when I was 6 for about 2 months.

I spent an entire summer in Idaho when I was 9 with my aunt/uncle and cousin.

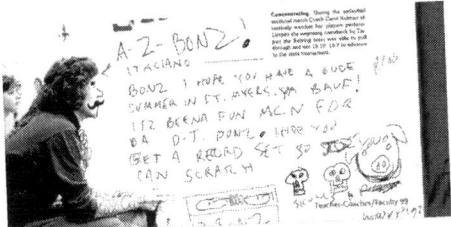

Greg's signature in my freshman yearbook.. we had a sort of a coded language that close friends tend to have.

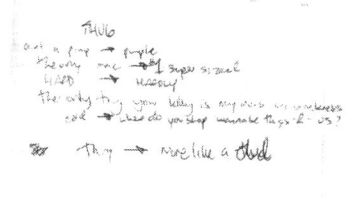

I had no idea what I was doing in my first promo shot, why I'm on a dirty beach in front of dock trying to look hard is beyond me.

I had been jotting down notes for my upcoming battles, the idea was if they said one thing I had a rebuttal for that ready.

Grad night my senior year.. We all stayed up all night and I was so exhausted I went into the girls bathroom at the Perkins we all went to eat at for breakfast.

I made spearfish out of duct tape a knife and a broom handle... but man how skinny am I in 7th grade?

I guess I've always been hammin it up for the camera.

I thought my ticket to college was football, God + my genetics had other plans.

I was really into bball until I got cut from my sophmore tryouts, I didnt really get tall till my senior year so my timing was terrible.

I was sprinkled when I was a catholic kid but when I was baptised at 15 it meant a lot more,.. (after I came to Christ).

Gallery | 123

GALLERY

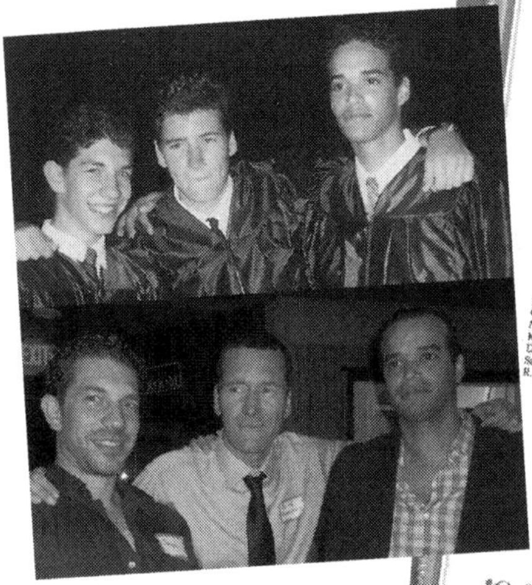

Then and Now class of 93.

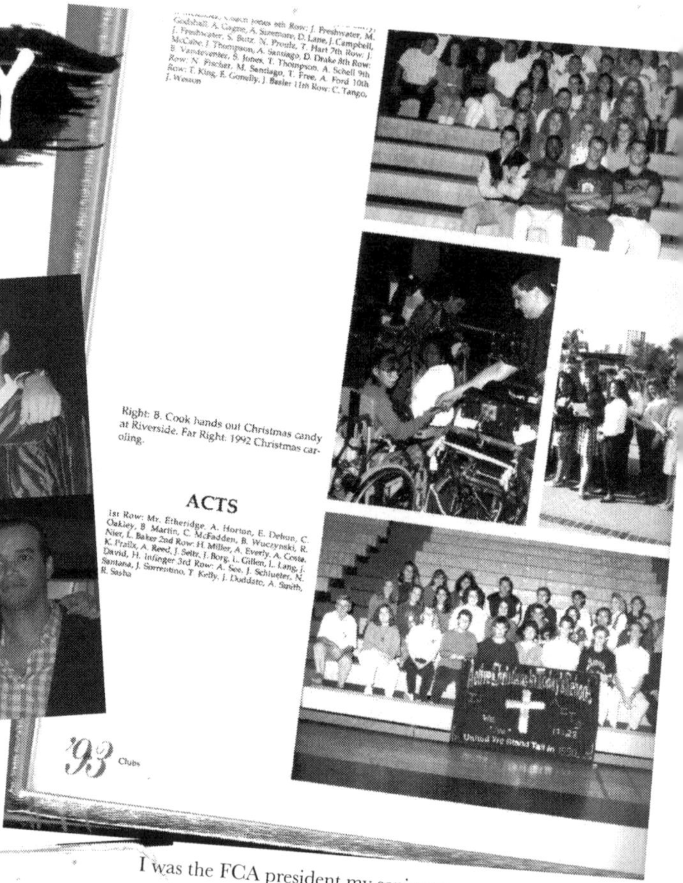

'93 Clubs

I was the FCA president my senior year.

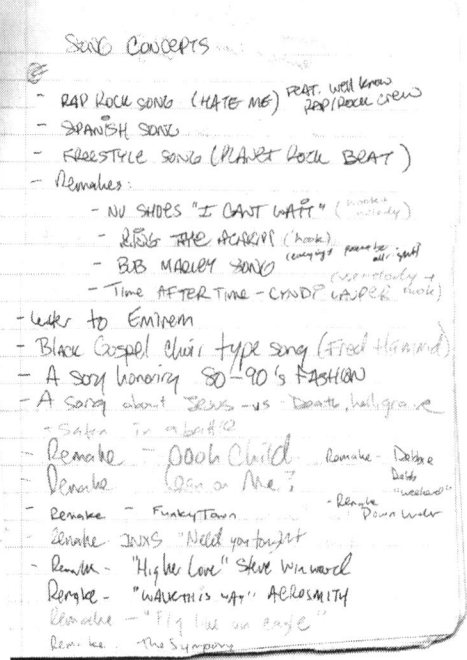

More song concepts I had scribbled down in 2001.

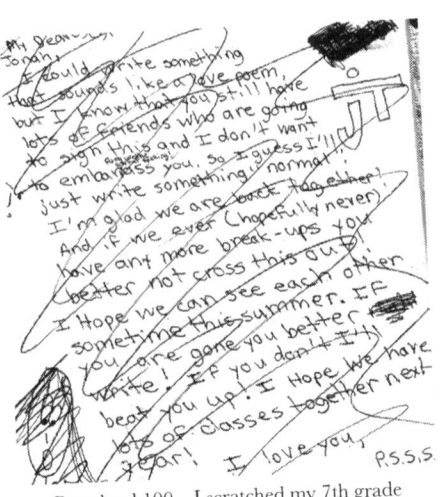

Petty level 100... I scratched my 7th grade girlfriends signature out after one of our many breakups .. sorry to where ever you are today.

124 | What Happened Was...

My favorite signature in my yearbook is that "You're the best dancer, you dress well and you tell me about God" - ha.. that sums up my life mission right there.

My first graff piece... aesthetically terrible on so many levels .. but I show it to let you know that we all start somewhere.

My grades were great until jr high then they plummeted, by the time I hit high school I was already behind. I think I graduated with a 3.2gpa

Then and Now me and Christa.

A very special thank you goes out to all my Kickstarter backers that helped make this book possible... you are appreciated!

Lance Kirkman, Amancay Maahs,

The Creative Fund, Destiney Michelle Wickle-Wackle Mishka Reeves, Haley Hodges,

Eric Escobedo, Kevin Tyler, Jeffrey Bytomski,

Matt Cox, Caleb Woods,

Terry Robison (my largest backer thank you Terry..),

John Stuart, Keith Windham, Paul DiSylvester,

Paul Pearson, Chad Bird, David Rathbun,

Jeffrey Everroad, Rose Barrosa,

Bradley Freedom Mason, Adam W. Duffy,

Raymond Doran, Shane Morris,

Michael Schnell, Nathanael Schenberg,

Josh Horner, Adam Blackstock,

Arend Maatkamp, Samuel Nosek,

John D. Miller III, Chris Clanton,

John Herring, Preston Housley,

Jackie Sampieri, Christine McCormick-DeVigili,

James Welbes, Shawn Deal,

Sean Brennan, Colton Everett Smith, Jonathan,

Scottie Stiles, Rebecca Pooler,

Joel Zink, Brandon & Arielle Carlson,

George Litten, Marko Schrader, Isaac Blanco,

Lyle Baker, Devin, Carisa McMillen,

John Hurskainen, Caleb Ashbaucher,

Jasmine Klugh, Shane Edwards, Tiff,

The Virkler Fam, Ian Jones, R. Mansfield,

Chris B, Scott Spaulding, CJ Burroughs,

Josh Crans, Randy Booth, Obie Pinner,

Jordan C Rostorfer, Kevin Burroughs, Silas, Dhiren,

Russell Morrison, Saymo'K, Miriam White,

Kathy Spillar, Dan Gilmer, Vince Tafoya,

Rachel Harris, Realizer, Mike Sisson,

Julie Crooks, Brian Blackmore, Morgan Matthew

Grant, Jonathan Calles, Tim Foley, Jack Germick,

Anita Davis, Rodney Neal, Jonathan Perez,

jwDRIGGS, Michael Freeman, Scott Triezenberg,

Tannah Wilson, Chris Nelson,

Makenzi Markham, V. Rose, Matt Smith,

Catherina Gaynor, ChuckieJ, Tucker T Dansie,

Smith Fedako, Jered Gering, Landon Bell,

Carter Taylor, Benjamin Matteson, Jack,

Grandma Patti, Kurt Green, Jake Palomaki, Alicia

& Chris Alexander, AJ Chapman,

Michael Mitchell, Kevin Bordner, Tim Smith,

Horacio Perez, Jaron "Jarodactyl" Cox, Will L,

Ian Jones, Joshua Belter, Estella Smith,

Laura Crandall, T. Pittman, Tom Valletto,

Ryan Liddell, Aaron West, KJ Ellington, Zak Mirzadeh, Tom Diehl, Fly Jello, Doug Stephens, Richard Mesa, Sarah Smith, Luke Chapman, Josh Evans, Aaron Springsteen, Ryland, Tom Moore, Kelly Roush, Jospeh Overby, Jeff McLaughlin, Stacie, Taylor Anderson, Abby "Abbsteroni" K, Mike Meador, John Michael Howell, Connor Patton, Scott Borgert, Darren Ray Green aka Stud Muffin, Reina, Keith Deugan, Miranda Morey, Ephancy, Cristina, Nathaniel Kelly, zadowsmash, Jonathan Coker, Jim Hopkins, Tyson Daniel Freshour, Brad da Emcee, Brenna Kate Simonds, Cyndi Baxter, Jesse Phillips, Andy Foster, Heath Landreth, Liliana Williams, Milton Robins, Darin Franklin, Nathan Neal, Cassandra Lee Craigo, Daniel Blair, Nathan Filyk, Sam Blackwell, Obie Pehm, Candice, Becca Doss, Toddulus Lindstrom, Ike Jay, Mark Petitt, Jonathan Schutz, James Tatum, Janney Carter, Dustin Bentley, Christopher Brady, C Scott S, David Gray, Donnie Sevy, Sketch the Journalist, Shawna Winney, Joshua Smith, Daniel Arnold, Jason, Shaabyi Gage, Torri Spierling, Ortheus Draughan, Timothy Love, Mitch Darrell, Shane Wingo, Chris Darland, Scott Spaulding, Michael Smith, Stephanie Davis, Lindsay Lyons, Jason "SA" Torres, Crystal Tittle, Shawn Beavers, Adam Burnett, Carl Peace, Eric Yaple, The BRB, R. Bruce Robidou, Sherry A. Yatich, Christopher Watson, Jono, Charles Satterfield, Devin Christian, Russell Reihart, My cousins Mary & Bobby Sorrentino, John Davies, Jonathan Eaton, Michaylah Malone, Jeremy Brown, J. Ely, Noah Gaskins, Scott Johnson, Judah Sloan, Timothy Cobb, Andrew Abdale, Jeffrey Behnke, Lee Denton, Sven Rafferty, Cory Laughlin, Keri Tegtmeier, Calvin Cpd Witt, Timothy Lanham, Michael Augustyniak, Talon Diwisch, Eigenhuis, Michael May, Sabrina Cooper, Scott Cohoon, Joseph Dizzy Eckhart, Kimberly Stone, Perry Hotter, Deb Church, Patricia & Tim Rench, Rebecca Johnson, Derek Bohn, M.A.P Gilea, Maddie, Abigail, Princeton, Gilea, Cantin, T-J Mohr, Dave Dittmaier, Kyle Penning, Betty Leppert, Royal Ruckus, Scott Jaramillo ~

"KJs2"

Made in the USA
Columbia, SC
06 June 2019